INDIAN ARTS **OF THE** SOUTHWEST

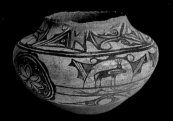

Rio Nuevo Publishers®
P.O. Box 5250, Tucson, Arizona 85703-0250
(520) 623-9558, www.rionuevo.com

Text and photography copyright © 1998, 2008 by Susanne and Jake Page. Drawings
by Jake Page. First edition (titled *Field Guide to Southwest Indian Arts and
Crafts*) 1998; Rio Nuevo Publishers edition (Indian Arts of the Southwest) 2008.

On the front cover: Hopi basket by unknown artist, Third Mesa style; necklace by
Angie Reano Owen, Santo Domingo; redware wedding vase by Celestina Naranjo,
Santa Clara; Zuni corn maiden by Richard Quam Jr. On the back cover: wicker
plaque by unknown artist, Hopi; storyteller by Helen Cordero, Cochiti; weaving by
Emma Roan, Navajo. Shown on page 1: Zuni pot, 1890s, artist unknown; page 3:
storyteller by Leonard and Mary Trujillo, Cochiti; page 5: pipestone snake by
Darren Shebola, Zuni; mosaic earring by Charlene Sanchez Reano and Frank
Reano, Santo Domingo; and burden basket signed "Enfield," Western Apache.

Library of Congress Cataloging-in-Publication Data

Page, Susanne.
[Field guide to Southwest Indian arts and crafts]
Indian arts of the Southwest / Susanne and Jake Page.
        p. cm.
Originally published: Field guide to Southwest Indian arts and crafts. New
York : Random House, c1998.
Includes bibliographical references and index.
ISBN 978-1-933855-17-2
1. Indian art—Southwest, New—Guidebooks. 2. Indians of North
America—Material culture—Southwest, New—Guidebooks. 3. Indians of North
America—Southwest, New—History—Guidebooks. 4. Southwest,
New—Antiquities—Guidebooks. 5. Southwest, New—Guidebooks. I. Page,
Jake. II. Title.
E78.S7P34 2007
704.03'97079—dc22

                                2007023220

Design: Karen Schober, Seattle, Washington.

Printed in Korea.

10   9   8   7   6   5   4   3   2   1

INDIAN ARTS
OF THE
SOUTHWEST

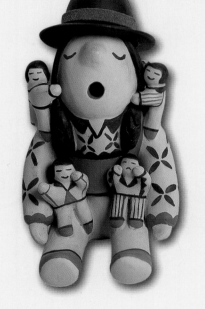

SUSANNE AND JAKE PAGE

RIO NUEVO PUBLISHERS
TUCSON, ARIZONA

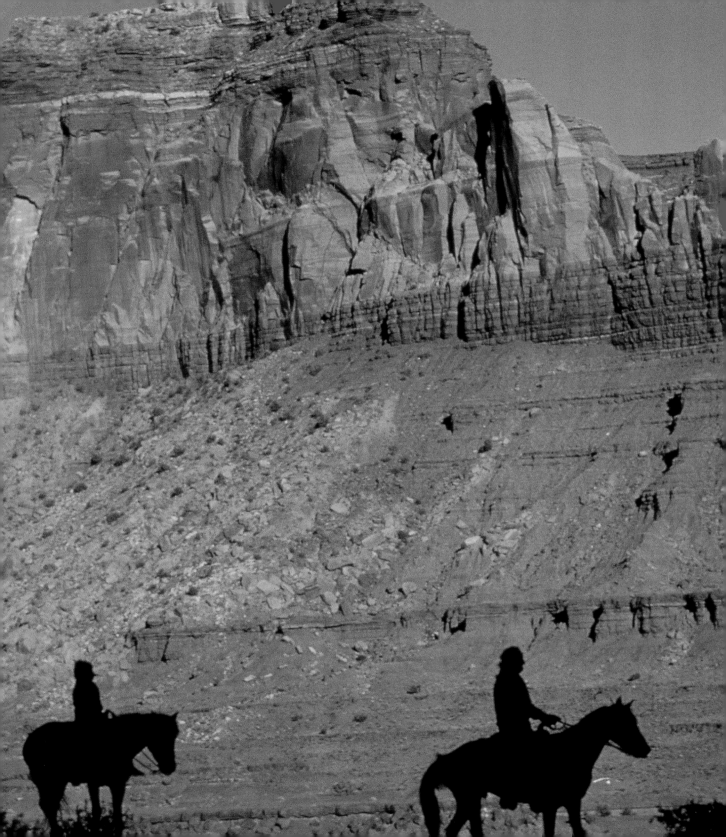

CONTENTS

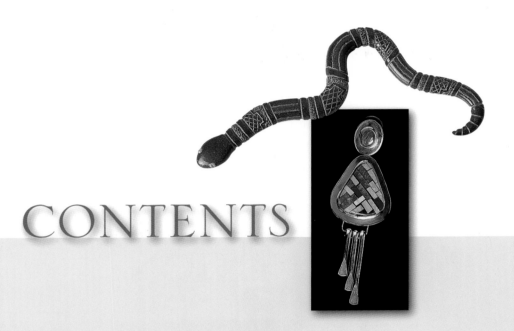

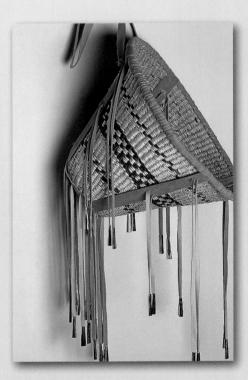

1 INTRODUCTION   6

   THE LAND   15

   PREHISTORY   17

   SOUTHWEST TRIBAL GROUPS TODAY   20

2 WEAVING   31

3 CARVINGS   41

4 POTTERY   54

5 BASKETRY   85

6 JEWELRY   100

7 VISITING THE INDIAN VILLAGES   122

   ACKNOWLEDGMENTS   129

   SUGGESTED READING   131

   INDEX   134

CHAPTER ONE

INTRODUCTION

Blackware figurine by Dorothy and Paul Gutierrez, Santa Clara.

THE ARRAY OF CRAFT OBJECTS that artisans of the many Indian tribes of the American Southwest offer to the world is astonishing in its variety and beauty—and for a newcomer it can be a bewildering kaleidoscope. To enter a gallery or store in the Southwest or elsewhere that specializes in these objects is to be confronted with a colorful, and at first confusing, realm of baskets, pots, figurines, jewelry, weavings, and other items. The wares are all recognizably "Indian," just as a forest or an aviary is recognizably full of a variety of birds. But what then? This book, somewhat like a field guide to birds, is designed first and foremost to help people identify what is in such an array—to help them become familiar with the characteristics that distinguish one tribe's traditional craft objects and designs from another's.

Beyond straightforward identification (an important first step to a deeper appreciation), this book has other goals and uses. It provides a basic introduction to the tribes of the American Southwest and the cultural traditions from which their arts and crafts have arisen;

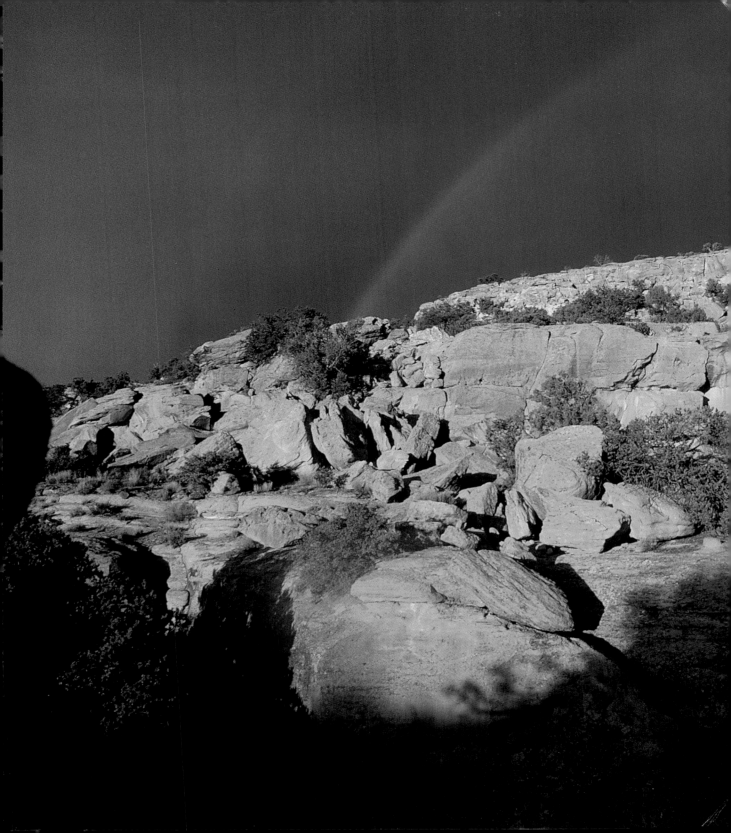

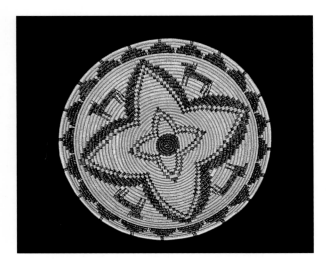

Western Apache basket, 1920s, artist unknown.

information about the techniques and materials these skilled artisans use; and guidance about visiting the tribes on their own lands. In addition, the book points out some signs of excellence within craft traditions, as well as signs of imitations (of which there are many), and it provides many other details geared to increase the reader's familiarity with, and appreciation of, the objects themselves, of the traditions they embody, and of the people who have made them.

Yet this is at best an introduction. Those seeking a deeper and more extensive understanding than any single introductory book can provide are extremely fortunate. The sheer quantity of books and pamphlets and museum exhibits (never mind scholarly treatises) about the arts and crafts of the Indian Southwest is probably unparalleled. No other region of Indian America—past or present—has been more thoroughly dug, studied, documented, analyzed, and celebrated. We have included lists of references, particularly those concerning the region's crafts, but also more general references to regional Indian history and culture.

In short, our intent is to provide an open and welcoming door to the rich and many-chambered house embodied in the works of these skilled people who are devoted to the continuation of traditions and art forms that have arisen from, and still bespeak, the core of their experience as members of unique worlds.

Some readers may be surprised at the free use of the word "Indian" in these pages, but in this region most native people are perfectly accepting of the conventional term. They will explain that they have their own tribal terms for themselves (Navajos, for example, call themselves "Diné," meaning "the People"), and most are sanguine about what the rest of the world calls them. Indeed, at various Indian events, such as rodeos and powwows, one will find plenty of pickups bearing bumper stickers that say "I'm Hopi Indian and Proud of It." Or Navajo or Zuni or what have you. In this region the older term is more common than "Native American"—as in the Southwestern Association for Indian Arts (SWAIA) or the Indian Arts and Crafts Association (IACA), two native organizations that support excellence and authenticity in this field.

WHO AND WHAT?

What, exactly, is meant here by the Southwest, and which tribes are included in it? For the purposes of this guide, we have with one exception (the Paiutes) followed the lead of the Smithsonian Institution's multivolume *Handbook of North American Indians* and focused on most of the tribes of Arizona and New Mexico, most notably the Navajo, Hopi, Zuni, and the numerous Pueblo tribes located along the upper reaches of the Rio Grande, and the O'odham of southern Arizona.

In using the term "arts and crafts" we are speaking primarily about largely *anonymous* traditions embodied in culturally *typical* forms. For example, Hopi pottery is traditionally done by women living in the four Hopi villages of First Mesa. (It is not traditionally done by men or by women from the villages of the other two Hopi mesas, where basketry is the craft of choice—but there are some male potters and some potters from the other mesas.) Most of these First Mesa Hopi women, and the others, create pottery from much the same materials using similar techniques and produce many of the same shapes and designs. That such a *tribal* tradition is, in one sense, anonymous does not mean that the work of each craftsperson is not unique; it simply means that the overall similarity of the work is more immediately apparent than any individual artistry. At any given time, individuals always shine above others artistically. In recent times some have inaugurated whole traditions or have come to excel within existing ones, and we take note of many of them.

But we have tended to include items that are first and foremost tribal—part of a collective tradition, distinct from work where an individual's particular style is more important than the body of tribal tradition. We admit at the outset that this distinction is a slippery slope, one that we have tumbled about on in deciding what to include. An excellent reference on this issue, if you can find a copy, is Lois and Jerry Jacka's *Beyond Tradition* (now out of print).

In addition, many Indians today have careers as "fine" artists—painters, engravers, lithographers, sculptors, and so forth. Many, if not all, of these artists make use of traditional tribal images and themes, but their work is not within the scope of this book.

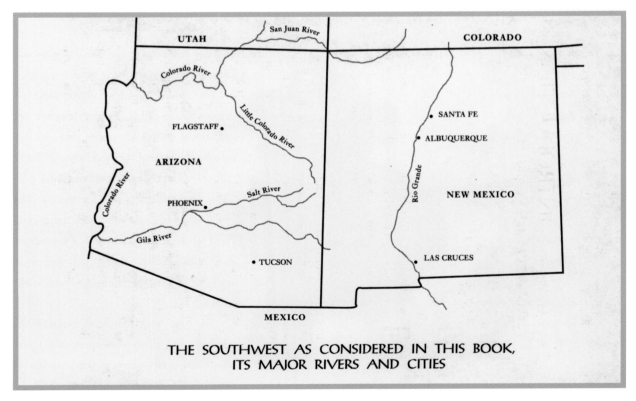

THE SOUTHWEST AS CONSIDERED IN THIS BOOK, ITS MAJOR RIVERS AND CITIES

At the other end of this spectrum, a great deal of material sold in the Southwest could be called "folk art" (as opposed to traditional crafts that arise from cultural use). Beyond that is material that could frankly be called "knickknacks." We mean the kind of thing—such as paintings on velvet, plaster animals, or dream-catchers—that may have been cranked out by Indians (or not) or machines (or not) but has never been made for anything but commerce. Such objects are found in numerous shops and roadside emporiums, and play no authentic cultural role.

This guide, then, focuses on authentic arts and crafts that are commonly encountered and continue to be made. These fall mostly into five craft types: woven textiles, figurines (including katsina dolls), pottery, basketry, and jewelry. These are the most characteristic of the Southwest tribes in general and the most often collected.

An important aspect of the beauty and charm of these craft objects has to do with the spirit in which they are made. This was explained to us once by the late Mary Toya of the Jemez Pueblo, a fine and productive maker of storyteller figurines, along with her daughters and sisters. "When we're making these for our own use," she said, "we sing our own traditional songs and prayers, and they become part of the thing we're making. But we know a lot of white people like hymns, so when we're making these things for them, we sing some of those old hymns." In this sense, no authentic Indian craft object is merely an inert thing of beauty.

A CAVEAT CONCERNING IMITATIONS AND FAKES

Along with the flourishing market for Indian arts and crafts, there has been a flourishing market for imitations and outright fakery—especially so-called Indian jewelry. No traditional craft is left out of this unfortunate trade. Each of the sections on individual crafts in this book contains advice on how to avoid fakes and imitations. The best way is to know what questions to ask, and we have included such questions in each craft section, along with points of excellence to look for within the realm of the authentic.

We have been fortunate to glean the wisdom of many knowledgeable and respected gallery owners and traders as well as the Indian Arts and Crafts Asso-

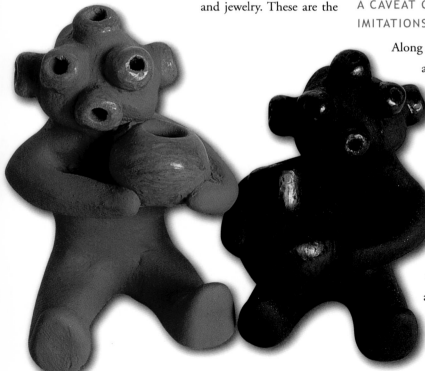

Redware and blackware Mudhead figurines, Dorothy and Paul Gutierrez, Santa Clara.

ciation, an organization of artisans and sellers devoted to promoting the health of the Indian arts and crafts world. Their advice is uniform: *ask questions and get documentation*. Any legitimate seller should provide a buyer with a receipt specifying what the piece is made of and confirming that it was handmade by an American Indian—and of what tribe. Federal law specifies that any item sold as Indian- or Native American-made must be the creation of an individual who is a member of a state or federally recognized tribe, or is tribally certified as an Indian artisan. If a dealer or private individual will not provide such documentation, walk away, just as you would from someone selling you a Rolex watch on a street corner—or the deed to a well-known bridge in New York City—who won't vouch for it. If a seller is discovered putting false information on such a receipt, under federal law he is subject to a fine of $250,000 and jail time: few will take the risk.

Until recently, fakes tended to be flimsy and poorly made. But the imitators have become more sophisticated, as have their products, and it is well worth becoming a bit of a connoisseur. Navajo rugs have been knocked off by innumerable pretenders, the most noted currently being the Zapotecs of Mexico. At the same time, many—including some Navajos—have palmed off katsina dolls as authentic Hopi creations.

More insidious, however, is the flood of foreign-made copies of Indian arts and crafts, especially jewelry, much of it produced in Asia. Some are of sufficient quality to be virtually indistinguishable from the originals by all but the most practiced eye. But they *are* almost always distinguishable by one factor: price. A very low price is a dead giveaway. If it seems too good to be true, it is.

Prices of legitimate Indian crafts vary, but you can get an excellent idea of the range from browsing in a reputable gallery and talking about what you see with the salespeople. A high-quality katsina doll will sell for $500 to $750 or more. Fifty dollars buys you a fake. A Zuni fetish necklace may sell for upwards of $1,500; no Zuni can make one for $100. Heishi, the shell beads made at Santo Domingo Pueblo for necklaces, may be priced at $20 or more a strand, while imports of machine-made beads may go for as little as $1 a strand (or, palmed off as the real thing, they may go for $20). Southwestern Indian-type basketry is now done in Pakistan (and often advertised in catalogs), and Romania has begun manufacturing and selling knockoffs of Taiwanese knockoffs of Indian jewelry. In almost every case, the prices of such items are less than what would be charged for authentic material. The items pictured in this book, by the way, run from $15 to $12,000. There is something authentic for every pocketbook.

Since the unwary often buy up "bargains" that are imitations, this trade shrinks the market for, and lowers the price of, the legitimate work of the tribes of the Southwest, thus diminishing and even eliminating the livelihood of thousands of people. As Mark Bahti of Bahti Indian Arts in Tucson and Santa Fe says, these are wholesalers "taking advantage of one impoverished culture to undercut another."

Most Indian artisans work at home, and they buy only the supplies they need for the short term. (Many will buy machine-made parts and assemble them. There is nothing wrong with this so long as the final piece is not labeled as handmade. Most other jewelry found in, say, department stores, is machine-made.) They do not have the economic power to buy materials like silver and stones in quantity and at wholesale prices or less, and many of them, once it is all computed, work at the minimum wage or less. But the minimum wage for an hour or two in the

United States may be a week's wages in the sweatshops of Far Eastern and other countries where fakes and imitations are made with materials bought in great quantity and at huge discounts.

These imported pieces are, by federal law, supposed to be labeled as such, and they usually are—with a paper sticker that is easily removed. There are stiff federal penalties for fobbing off imports and imitations as authentic, but plenty of unscrupulous people do it anyway. A town in the Philippines, for example, renamed itself Zuni so it could truthfully label its products "Made in Zuni." Federal enforcement of the laws on the books—notably by the Customs Service—is hamstrung by a lack of manpower, though efforts are under way to strengthen enforcement, as well as to close some loopholes. (For example, the current law says nothing about the importing of *components,* as opposed to whole pieces.)

Some tribes, in particular the Zuni and Navajo, have explored ways of certifying tribal artisans and trademarking their products so that they could sue anyone copying Zuni or Navajo designs and selling fake items. In 2006 the Zuni Cultural Arts Council passed the "Certification for Zuni Made Arts and Crafts Ordinance" as part of this ongoing effort to protect the work of Zuni artisans.

As noted, each craft section of this book provides hints and clues from the experts on separating the imitation from the authentic, along with questions anyone should ask of a salesperson—Indian or non-Indian. To quote Mark Bahti again, "The only dumb question is the one you didn't ask."

There is yet one more caveat: a commonly seen sign on many roadside emporiums and "Indian villages" as well as urban stores advertises prices for Indian crafts that are *50% off!*—and sometimes more. In virtually every case, the retailer establishes the price at twice the going rate, then takes away half. It isn't illegal, or even immoral. It's simply a marketing charade. (Exceptions to this rule are those wholesalers who also will sell wholesale to the public, including Palms Trading Company in Albuquerque.)

This book is designed to familiarize you with the real thing in Southwest Indian arts and crafts and to steer you away from the false. There is nothing *wrong* with buying an imitation or reproduction, so long as you are aware of what it is. However, the assumption herein is that the reader not only wants the real thing but does not want to be hoodwinked to his or her own embarrassment and to the diminishment of the people who created these beautiful things in the first place.

HOW THIS BOOK IS ORGANIZED

In this book we explore five major categories of traditional art forms—textile weaving, carvings (specifically, fetishes and katsinas), pottery, basketry, and jewelry—and the people who make them. As each tribe appears for the first time, we also offer some brief insights into its history, culture, and way of life; for example, we discuss the Navajo people in greatest detail in our Weaving chapter, but only briefly when they come up again later in the Pottery, Basketry, and Jewelry chapters.

The heart of this book is the photography of craft objects, highlighting the features by which you can identify their tribal origins. Merely flipping through these pages can go a long way toward giving you a feel for this material—a sense of being in a familiar neighborhood in which one has an almost intuitive sense that this, say, looks Hopi or that

RIGHT: Wedding vase by Andrew Padilla, Laguna.

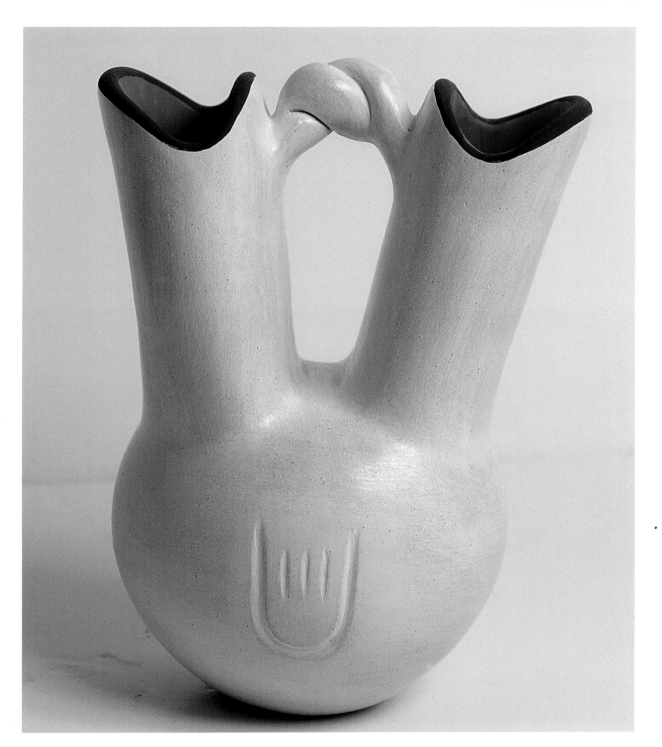

looks Zuni. The text also provides information about the craft items pictured—including details about local techniques and materials, along with tribal and cultural information. For example, the Hopi technique of overlay jewelry was introduced after World War II to provide returning veterans with a distinct handcraft to pursue. The text also includes specific qualities to look for within the overall craft. (To continue the Hopi jewelry example: one sign of excellence is the fineness of hand-stamping.)

In addition to a brief inclusion on the San Juan Paiutes, this book covers the works of four major groups,

Overlay bracelet by the late Emory Sekaquaptewa, Hopi.

tribes that are closely linked by either cultural style or language (or both): the pueblo-dwelling tribes; the Yuman-speaking peoples; the Pimas and Papagos of the southern Arizona deserts, who are now referred to as O'odham; and the Apaches and Navajos. You will find certain kinds of information on the role of crafts within a given tribe. For example, among the delightful bestiary of animal figurines carved for the trade by Zuni craftspeople, six animals in particular have a deep and ancient religious significance and are thus a doorway into the Zuni worldview.

It is useful to know the status of Indian lands and how to visit them. Here an overall etiquette exists—hardly different from any culture's good manners, but

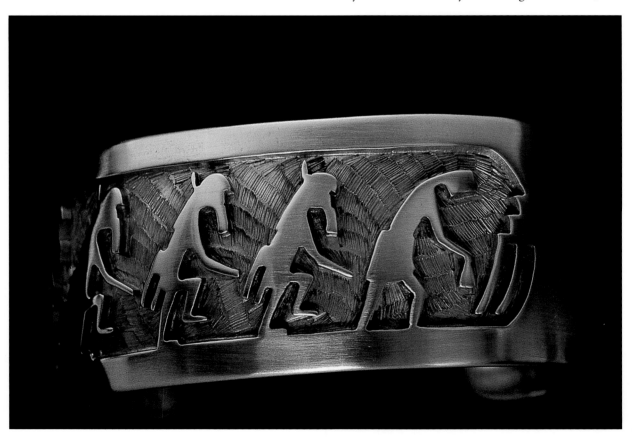

worth reviewing. Some of the tribes of the area have special customs and manners that a visitor should understand and, in the best of circumstances, be aware of when on tribal lands or among tribal people. Perhaps the most notable of these is the Navajo tendency not to stare at anyone or look directly into another's eyes. To do so is to offer a challenge; to look aside is a Navajo courtesy, as is a handshake that is soft and fleeting. Navajos always greet one another with a handshake.

The Southwest prides itself on being the land of "Three Cultures"—Indian, Hispanic, and the rest, which are lumped together as "Anglo." Of course, there are many groups of people in the Southwest who would prefer not to be thought of as Anglo, and there are as well many ways of being Hispanic. Each Indian tribe is itself a separate culture. The general Indian presence is indeed a major one in the Southwest; nowhere in the United States is it felt more strongly. There are many reasons for this, not the least of which is that the Indian cultures there have, for a variety of reasons, remained more intact than anywhere else.

It is useful to remember also that the tribes are, in a very real political sense, nations within the greater nation of the United States, with increasing exercise of sovereignty over their land and their own affairs, and with specific treaty or other reciprocal political ties with the United States government. In these ways, the Indian tribes of America differ from all its other ethnic aggregations.

By way of exercising this limited sovereignty, many Southwestern tribes operate gambling casinos on their reservation land. This is controversial in some quarters, but the casinos have provided money to the tribes—money that is most often spent on education, health care, and other areas that benefit the community. Little of it flows directly into the hands of individual members of the tribes, with the exception of those employed by the casinos. Some Indian casinos display and sell local arts and crafts, as do other tribal installations. Many of the Indian craftspeople rely on their artisanship for much, if not all, of their livelihood. On many of the Pueblo feast days, the villages are full of booths selling arts and crafts from other pueblos around the state, as well as food and cooling drinks. One handy way to get the exact dates of these feast days is from the Archdiocese of Santa Fe's website (www.archdiocesesantafe.org).

THE LAND

The Indians of the Southwest today inhabit several million acres of reservation land in the modern states of Arizona and New Mexico and a sliver of Utah. They were once the exclusive inhabitants of the entire region, an area that, for purposes of this volume, is defined by the river systems of the southern half of the Colorado and the northern half of the Rio Grande.

This is an area with an arid climate—receiving, throughout most of it, between three and twelve inches of precipitation annually, some in the form of winter snow in northern areas, with far more rain and snow in more mountainous areas. Less objectively, the Southwest is where the light of the sun has an indescribable vibrancy.

The Southwest includes three different kinds of deserts among its ecological systems. One is the "green" Sonoran Desert in southern Arizona, with its huge saguaro cacti and two annual rainy seasons—this is a subtropical desert where it rarely freezes. Another is the Chihuahuan Desert of southern and middle New Mexico, with one rainy season, hot summers but very cold winters, and a less diverse plant life characterized by creosote bush and yucca. These two desert types exist mostly in valleys

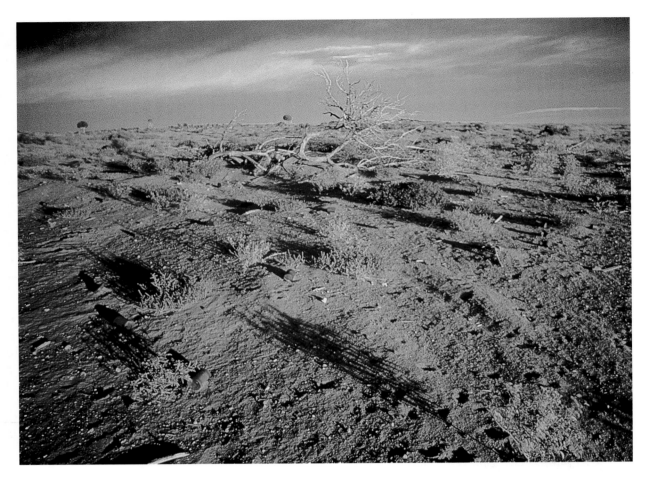

between jagged, north-south running mountain chains—
what is called basin and range country. The third type, the
Great Basin Desert, is chiefly scrubby oceans of sage and
almost without cactus. It extends from the Colorado
Plateau as far north as Oregon. In fact, there is a fourth
desert type: California's Mojave Desert reaches into western Arizona, an extremely hot and dry desert characterized by sparse vegetation that is dominated by yucca.

In addition to desert, a distinct, jumbled mountainous area extends in a swath through the middle of
the region—a highland given over to evergreen forest
and cold mountain streams. In the north lies the Colorado Plateau, a huge, high plate of the earth characterized by mesa lands, a few high peaks and mountain
ranges, and thousands of canyons, the largest of which
is Grand Canyon, etched over the millennia into the
plateau's rock.

Elevation varies in this region from a low of some 1,000
feet above sea level to more than 12,000 feet. Generally,
temperature falls the higher one goes, and the result is a
fairly precise layering of life zones, from the cacti of low
desert lands through dwarf forests of piñon pine and juniper
to parklands of ponderosa pine, followed by Canadian-type
forests of spruce and finally a few treeless alpine summits.

PREHISTORY

Into this enormous and amazingly diverse landscape and over many thousands of years, people have come, many leaving behind only silent ruins and artifacts, others with descendants among today's tribes. Essentially the prehistoric residents fall into two broad categories: those who tended to settle along or near sources of water that permitted a sedentary agricultural life, and those who settled the lands in between, especially the mountain areas, living chiefly as semi-nomadic hunters and gatherers. Most of today's tribes derive from the agricultural peoples who have been in this region for millennia. The hunter-gatherer cultures include some recent arrivals—people of Athapaskan origins in the far north who reached these parts about A.D. 1400 and became the several Apache tribes and the Navajos.

The cultural adjustments all these people had to make are, not surprisingly, reflected in their craft objects, which, taken together, are essentially tool kits of a domestic or spiritual nature—or both. (Among such people, the distinction between religious and secular practices has never been sharp.) The tools used by people who lead a more settled life in villages surrounded by fields of food crops are predictably more diverse and more elaborate than those of a band that must carry its belongings to seasonal hunting and gathering grounds.

Archaeologists have plumbed the human settlements and cultures of this region more thoroughly than those of any other in the nation, tracing them back more than 10,000 years to early hunters and gatherers who stalked woolly mammoths with arrows tipped with fluted points

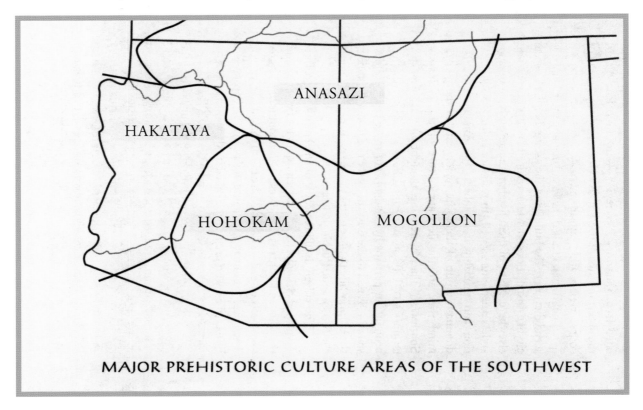

ANASAZI

HAKATAYA

HOHOKAM

MOGOLLON

MAJOR PREHISTORIC CULTURE AREAS OF THE SOUTHWEST

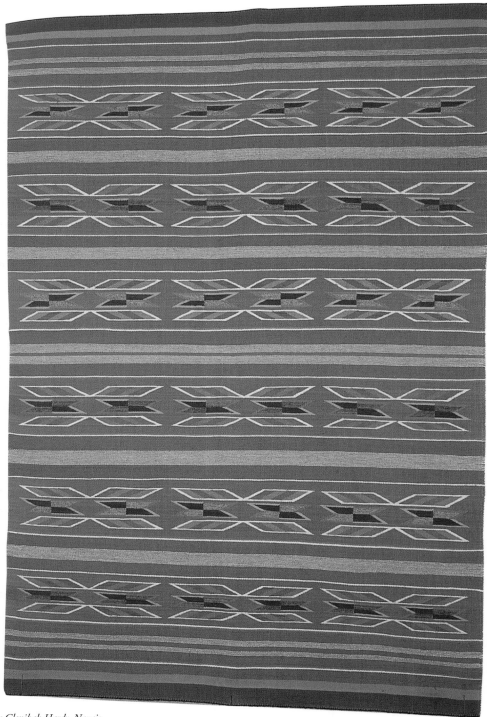

Crystal rug by Glenibah Hardy, Navajo.

(archaeologists named these cultures for places like Clovis and Folsom, where arrow tips were found). By 2000 B.C., rudimentary agriculture, imported from what is now Mexico, was practiced by people who lived in pit houses in more sedentary settlements. Succeeding cultures have been characterized by increasingly sophisticated craft objects as well as settlement patterns (in some instances referred to specifically by their crafts, such as Basket Maker II and III).

Among the crafts we are concerned with here, baskets have been found dating back as early as 6000 B.C. Weaving, along with stone pendants and ornaments of bone and shell, appears as early as 2000 B.C., as do the beginnings of pottery. This is about the time a primitive type of maize was introduced, though it was not to become a major factor in agriculture and diet for another 2,000 years.

Lidded basket by Frances Stevens, Tohono O'odham.

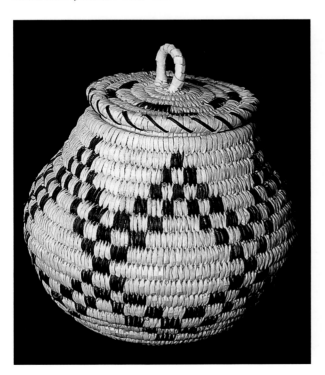

In about A.D. 1100, four major cultural areas flourished in the Southwest. Each was characterized by distinct craft objects related to its specific environment and way of life. All of these cultural groups were influenced by one another to some degree, often borrowing techniques and styles, particularly at the edges of their territories, thus making the archaeologist's task all the more challenging. Also, the existence of non-indigenous items such as macaw feathers is proof that the people of one region were not altogether isolated from those of other regions—the American plains, the desert uplands of present-day Utah and Nevada, and of course Mexico and Central America.

The **Anasazi** (called the Hisatsinom by their Hopi descendants) were the builders of the astoundingly elaborate city-like installations at Mesa Verde, Chaco Canyon, and elsewhere. Many of them lived in smaller outlying pueblo-style settlements as well. In terms of cultural sophistication and probably in numbers, the Anasazi were the dominant group of the entire region, and in the popular mind they are the defining culture of the prehistoric Southwest. They were long thought to have vanished around A.D. 1300 in some inexplicable disappearing act, brought on perhaps by drought, but more recent understanding is that to the west they gave rise to at least some of the Hopi, while to the east they gave rise to at least some of the Rio Grande Pueblo peoples.

The village-dwelling people of the **Hohokam** culture developed elaborate irrigation techniques for farming along the Gila and Salt Rivers in present-day southern Arizona, eventually extending their culture north almost to Flagstaff. They are, presumably, survived today by the Papago and Pima tribes, who prefer to be called by their own names for themselves: Tohono O'odham and Akimel O'odham.

The **Mogollon** culture developed a pueblo-style life in the mountainous areas of southern New Mexico and eastern Arizona; it vanished, perhaps becoming absorbed into Anasazi culture. In any event, the culture and its most notable artifacts, pottery decorated in the distinctively whimsical style called Mimbres, ceased to exist.

The people of the **Hakataya** culture tended toward a mobile life lived in temporary homes that were often walled

Necklace of spiny oyster shell, turquoise, and machined coral beads, by Angie Reano Owen, Santo Domingo.

with rock and situated along well-established trails. They produced only the bare necessities in terms of tools. This was a hunter-gatherer culture that presumably gave rise to the Yuman tribes in today's Arizona, including the Havasupai, Yavapai, and Hualapai (sometimes spelled Walapai).

SOUTHWEST TRIBAL GROUPS TODAY
THE PUEBLO TRIBES

Pueblo is Spanish for "village." The Spanish found many permanent settlements ranged across the Colorado

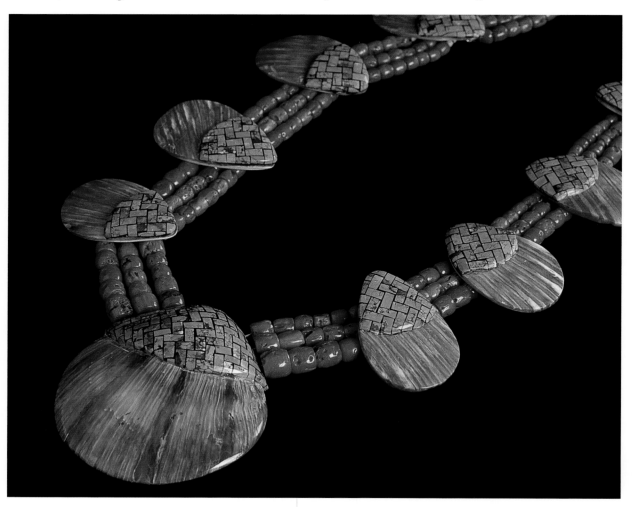

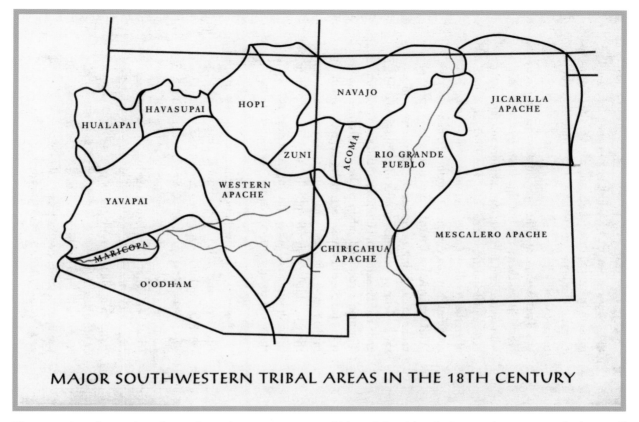

MAJOR SOUTHWESTERN TRIBAL AREAS IN THE 18TH CENTURY

Plateau and to the south and east, from the westernmost Hopi, in northeastern Arizona, to the major concentration associated with the Rio Grande in New Mexico. Each tribe inhabited one or more compact towns with houses of stone or adobe (mud brick) ranged around plazas, all were engaged in intensive agriculture linked to a complex ceremonial life, and all produced a distinct range of crafts. Each pueblo contained several ceremonial chambers called *kivas,* which were usually underground and were entered by ladders through the roof.

Many of the Pueblo cultures the Spanish came upon remain geographically and culturally intact to a remarkable degree, jealously guarding their lifeways and religious practices in spite of the arrival of the Roman Catholic faith and Spanish rule (to one degree or another), as well as other and later intrusions.

A defining moment in Pueblo-Spanish relations was the Pueblo Revolt of 1680 when, under the leadership of a shadowy figure called "Pope" from the San Juan Pueblo, most of the tribes from Taos to Hopi and up and down the Rio Grande joined forces, killed priests, destroyed mission churches, and drove some 3,000 Spanish colonists out of the territory to El Paso. This is the only war American Indians can be said to have won.

Twelve years later the Spanish returned in force and reestablished their rule, but this was a less severe regime, with secular and religious leaders more tolerant of Pueblo ceremonial and traditional life. The Pueblos, before and after the revolt, were subject as well to raiding by surrounding Navajos, Apaches, Comanches, Paiutes, and Utes. With the arrival of United States rule in 1848, much of the raiding ceased, but thereafter the people were subject to the sometimes well-meaning but often misguided interference and assistance of both federal and state governments. Through treaty and other reciprocal arrangements, the tribes have been accorded a growing degree of sovereignty in the past century and a half, and their original cultures—though added to significantly by such introductions as Spanish sheep and silversmithing, American political notions and pickup trucks—remain, on the whole, astoundingly intact.

Anthropologically, those Pueblos to the west (particularly Hopi and Zuni) are matrilineal societies with membership in a clan being a major part of one's tribal identity. To the east, in the upper Rio Grande, Pueblos are patrilineal societies given over less to clans than to membership in what are called "moieties," tribal subdivisions associated usually with summer and winter. Many Pueblos exhibit some combination of these two social structures. Almost all include a strong tradition of "clowns," figures who play a role that is both amusing and morally instructive, and in some of the more eastern tribes the clowns, called *Koshare* and *Quirana,* play a highly significant priestly role.

Except in the two easternmost tribes (Taos and Picuris), katsinas are a major feature of religious life. These are the famous masked dancers who perform in public ceremonies and embody the spirits or essences of the many phenomena of nature. (We use the spelling *katsina* rather than *kachina,* as it is closer to the actual pronunciation.) The practice is best known in Zuni and Hopi pueblos. The other pueblos maintain a greater degree of privacy in this and other matters of a religious nature. The katsina

dances, highly religious affairs held outdoors and filled with color and sound, motion and prayer, in architecture that joins the earth to a vast overarching sky, have been called by Yale art historian Vincent Scully "the most profound work of art in North America."

In addition to a katsina society, most of the Pueblos have a complexly layered array of other religious or priestly societies with a variety of local functions. These tend, in the east, more to healing functions—ridding individuals of disease or the afflictions brought about by witchcraft—and in the west include other, esoteric functions. Much Pueblo ceremonialism is devoted to bringing timely rains to a dry climate. Where the people continue agriculture most intensely, their ceremonial life remains most intact.

Generally, four language groups exist among the Pueblos. The Hopi speak a Uto-Aztecan language related to those of the Shoshoneans of the north and certain Mexican tribes. The Zunis speak a language that is bafflingly unique and of unknown roots, though some evidence exists that it could have arisen in California. Several peoples in the approximate middle of Pueblo-land—including Cochiti, Santo Domingo, San Felipe, Santa Ana, Zia, Laguna, and Acoma—speak dialects of a language called Keresan (pronounced KER-i-sen), which is thought to have come from Anasazi roots in Chaco and Mesa Verde. A fourth language group, chiefly of the eastern Pueblos is Tanoan (the several subgroups are largely mutually unintelligible). Six of the northern pueblos—San Juan, San Ildefonso, Santa Clara, Nambe, Tesuque, and Pojoaque—share the Tewa language division of the Kiowa-Tanoan tongue, and much of the culture and history of all six conforms to a common pattern. The Tewa-speaking Pueblo peoples are descended from the Anasazi and Mogollon cultures, and trace their origins to one or another lake in what is now Colorado. From there, they migrated south to subsequent locations and finally to their current one along the Rio Grande. Residents of Taos, Picuris, Sandia, and Isleta speak Tiwa, and Towa is spoken at Jemez Pueblo.

The Pueblo people believe they emerged into this world from an earlier one—usually within the earth—and

see their tribal and personal role as part of a highly structured universe. Their creation stories (that is to say, their own history) long ago set down the rules and principles by which a proper life is to be lived in this universe. In theocratic societies such as these, few distinctions exist between the secular and the religious: one's personal existence is bound up in complex ways with the existence of one's people, and one's behavior is therefore scrutinized carefully by one's neighbors and leaders. The highly

Sandpainting rug by Luanna Tso, Navajo.

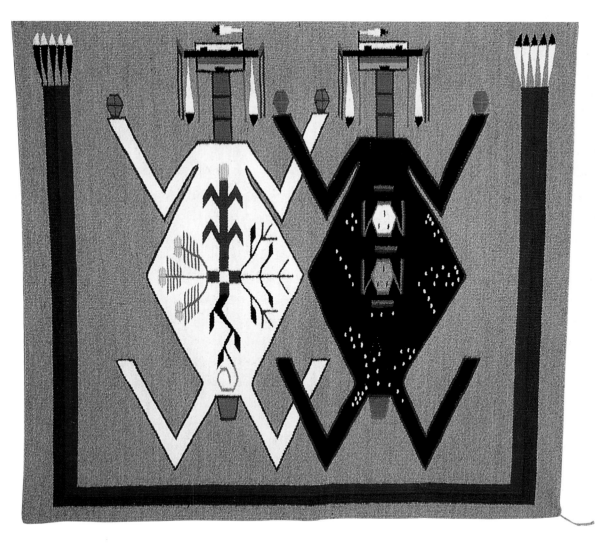

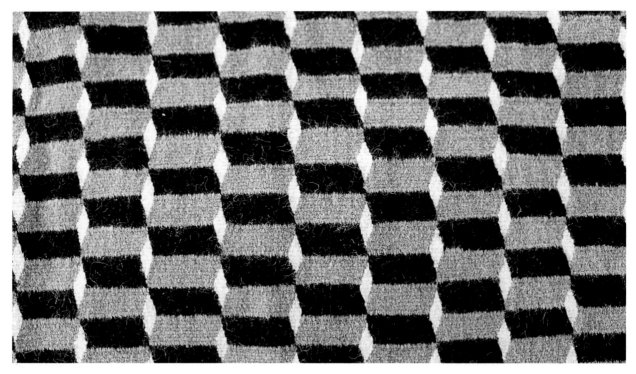

Weaving of undyed churro wool by Elsie Martinez, Navajo.

communal nature of such a life is at odds with the highly individualistic, even atomized, nature of American life, as well as with America's most notable characteristic—its cash economy. Each of the pueblos has struggled differently, and with varying goals and degrees of success, to accommodate such opposite ways.

Arriving in the late sixteenth century, the Spanish forced a number of features on the Pueblos' deeply ingrained social systems—notably, a secular governor for each pueblo, Roman Catholicism, and various new tools and foods, such as wheat. It was among these northern pueblos that the Spaniards established their own political center, and it was here that their influence was most forcibly pressed upon native populations. Indians were used for forced labor, and the Spanish attempted to suppress their religious practices.

When the Spanish returned to the region twelve years after the region-wide Pueblo Revolt of 1680, they practiced a more tolerant rule. Rather than replace native religions, for example, they simply added various Catholic practices, and to this day the two coexist quite comfortably. Through the period of Mexican rule (starting in 1821), life went on more or less without incident except for the tragic eruption of epidemics such as smallpox.

With American rule, beginning in 1848, came other pressures—missionary efforts, policies that took children from their villages and placed them in distant schools (where they were supposed to shed their Indian ways), tourism, and the immense magnet of the cash economy. Each of the pueblos has made its own accommodation to these forces. In addition, especially once various complex and longstanding matters having to do with land grants were arbitrated and settled, each pueblo has maintained neighborly relations with longtime Hispanic neighbors. For centuries, Spanish was commonly the second language (along with many other non-Tewa Indian tongues), but for the most part this has been replaced by English, in which most Pueblo people are fluent.

A pleasant door into the lifeways and crafts of the pueblos is to wander the halls off the Indian Pueblo Cultural Center, located one block north of Interstate 40 in Albuquerque at 2401 12th Street N.W.

THE YUMANS

For at least a thousand years, Yuman-speaking people have lived along the Colorado River and its tributaries and in the adjacent highlands of central Arizona. Due to the remoteness of their desert and semi-desert lands, they were little known to outsiders before the latter part of the nineteenth century. Scant archaeological work suggests that they lived throughout this long period of relative isolation hunting

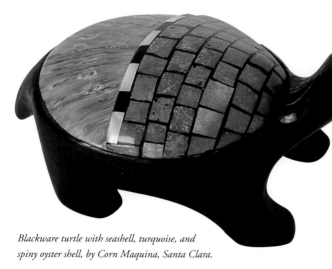

Blackware turtle with seashell, turquoise, and spiny oyster shell, by Corn Maquina, Santa Clara.

and gathering, and practicing a simple agricultural life—growing corn, beans, and gourds in river bottomlands.

For the most part, local groups and bands lived in rancheria-style aggregations, with low, rectangular, earth-covered houses some hundred yards apart. Tribal identity appears to have been strong—there was a great deal of intertribal warfare and a need for tribal defense against enemies such as the Navajos. At the same time, social organization was informal, with the household being the main component of life; in each settlement, there were certain men of prominence but with little authority. There was little formal ceremony, religious life being mostly shamanistic and devoted largely to healing, though certain shamans specialized in preparing warriors and hunters. Mourning ceremonies were commonly elaborate.

THE O'ODHAM

Known since Spanish times as the Pima and Papago, as mentioned earlier, these Uto-Aztecan-speaking people prefer to be called by their own names for themselves. *O'odham* means essentially "we, the people": the Pima being the Akimel O'odham (the river people) and the Papago the Tohono O'odham (the desert people). The two tribes are closely related and are more than likely descended from Hohokam cultures that thrived in southern Arizona in prehistoric times, making use of extensive irrigation agriculture.

THE APACHES AND NAVAJOS

At some point before A.D. 1500, and perhaps as much as 500 years earlier, groups of people began to arrive in the Southwest who had split off from the Athapaskan tribes of southern Alaska and northwestern Canada. They no doubt had made their way south along the great cordillera of the Rocky Mountains, and from there, to the west or east or both. In any event, they trickled in, continuing a life mostly of hunting and gathering in small groups. By the time of the Spanish arrival in the sixteenth century, Apachean people were found in the eastern half of Arizona, virtually all of New Mexico, and extending into the plains of present-day Oklahoma and Texas, as well as into northern Mexico, thinly scattered over vast tracts of land not already settled by earlier-arriving tribes. Probably from the very outset, these newcomers exerted a force in the Southwest far beyond what their mere numbers (never very great) would suggest.

In the region covered by this book, five distinct groupings of Apachean people came to live in the lands around the Pueblo people. In the north, approximately from Hopi to Taos, were the lands of what would become the Navajos,

Sifter basket, yucca on a willow ring, artist unknown, Hopi. Note the "SOS" in the center of the design.

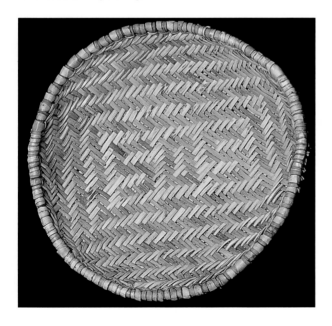

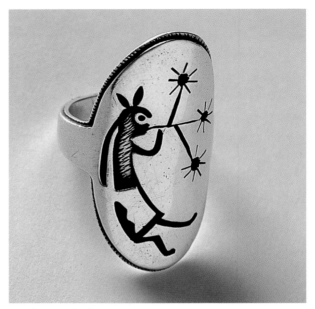

Ring by Victor Coochwytewa, Hopi.

a now-huge tribe with Apachean origins that gets its own separate treatment in this book. The northern half of eastern New Mexico was the home of the Jicarilla Apaches, whose lands extended northward well into Colorado as well. The Mescalero Apaches held sway in the southern half of eastern New Mexico, extending into Texas. West of the Rio Grande were the Chiricahuas, whose lands extended from the New Mexican mountain highlands into the deserts of Mexico and southeastern Arizona. And, in the highlands of Arizona, from the Salt and Gila rivers north to Hopi and Zuni, the Western Apaches roamed.

These were not tribes so much as geographical groupings that came to share certain distinct characteristics within a much larger, common way of life. This was characterized by the local group, a matrilineally based, extended family group of less than a hundred people, which followed game and wild food seasonally within a particular territory. Hunting was men's work, as was the fashioning of weapons; men also trained children in the ways of hunting, raiding, and warfare. Women were the gatherers of such food as nuts, and of firewood, and were the tanners of hides. Women also cared for children, erected the temporary houses called "wickiups," and made baskets and household utensils. All young Apaches, male and female, were trained to be self-sufficient in the wild, and many women were capable warriors.

Agriculture played a limited role among the Western Apaches, the Jicarillas, and the Navajos; the Mescaleros and particularly the Chiricahuas prided themselves on not practicing it. Navajos, of course, would take up the Spanish sheep and become preeminent pastoralists.

Apachean religion was (and is) chiefly shamanistic, devoted to curing various ills including those inflicted by witches (a pervasive fear), and women as well as men might be shamans and priests. A girl's puberty rite was (and is) a

"Grandmother" necklace by Doris and James Del Coriz, Santo Domingo.

major feature of Apache (and Navajo) ceremonial life, and most other rites were designed to intercede with the deities of nature (such as the Mountain Gods) for assistance.

Matrilineal clans, probably borrowed from Pueblo neighbors to the north, came into being among the Western and Chiricahua Apaches. A moiety system, also probably a borrowing from the northern Pueblos, appeared among the Jicarillas. The Navajos would take on certain Pueblo traits in many significant ways.

The local Apache groups were usually part of a recognizable band, normally led by a charismatic person whose leadership was not hereditary (the name Cochise remains perhaps the most widely known). Most of the economic and religious aspects of daily life were accomplished within the local group, men joining such a group by marriage and taking on wide responsibility for their in-laws. Extreme courtesy was called for between a man and his in-laws, this being most elaborate among the Chiricahuas. Mates were chosen from the band, which came together

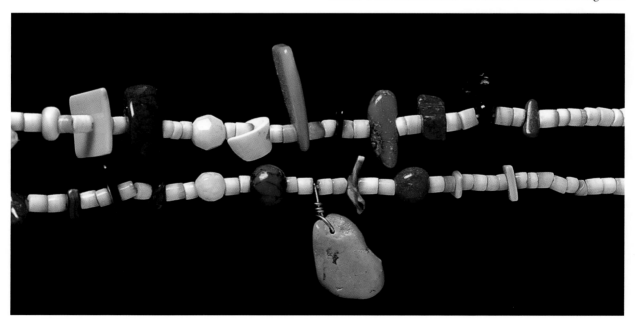

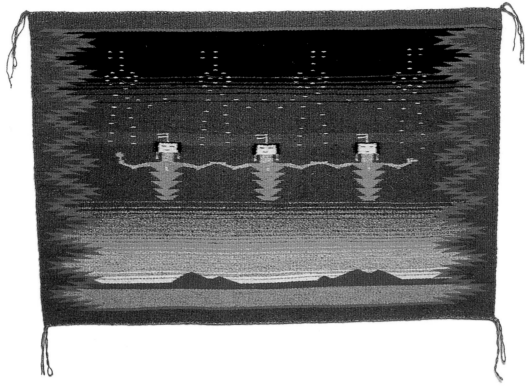

Yei-be-chei rug by Jaymes Henio, Navajo.

as needed for such purposes as raiding. (The Chiricahuas, for example, comprised only three such bands.)

All the Apaches practiced raiding of their more sedentary neighbors—taking food stores as well as women and children—and this increased with the arrival of the Spanish and their livestock, which provided attractive targets. Raiding, an important economic part of Apache life, was quite distinct from warfare, which was motivated by a felt need for vengeance or the protection of one's homelands from invasion. (Completely different ceremonies prepared raiders and warriors, and a raid was deemed totally successful only if nobody on either side was killed.) Apaches raided, and were raided by, the other Indians in their midst, those like Comanches on their outer borders, and by the Spanish settlers.

Throughout the centuries of Spanish rule in the American Southwest, the Apaches not only remained free of it, but largely determined where the Spanish themselves could settle. All Apaches quickly took to the Spanish horse. Raiding and hostilities became less and less distinguishable as Apaches fought fiercely to protect their lands wherever they were encroached upon, all the while raiding neighboring tribes, though sometimes forging temporary anti-Spanish leagues with them. Agreements, such as peace treaties, might be entered into by one Apache leader but had no force on neighboring bands, much less whole peoples.

When the United States gained titular hegemony over the region in 1848, this situation continued until the

U.S. Army rounded up the Apaches and placed them on reservations. In due course, this policy resulted in some of the most ferocious warfare ever seen before or since in the Southwest, during which the Apaches proved themselves among the most skilled guerrilla warriors in history.

The Chiricahuas were the last to give in—Geronimo and his renegade band of about fifty had withstood 5,000 U.S. Cavalry troops for two years before surrendering in 1886. (There were a few other holdouts.) The Chiricahuas—so-called "hostiles," others already located on reservations, and even those who had fought *with* the U.S. Cavalry—were rounded up and sent by train to prison camps in Florida. There, briefly in Alabama, and then in Fort Sill, Oklahoma, they were to remain prisoners of war for twenty-three years. Freed in 1913, some eighty elected to remain in Fort Sill on private allotted land, while the rest (some 120) elected to live among the Mescaleros on their reservation in southern New Mexico. They have since intermarried and largely lost whatever identity they had in any "tribal" sense as Chiricahuas, though individuals remain assertive and proud of their Chiricahua lineage.

Sandstone horse by Homer Warren, Navajo.

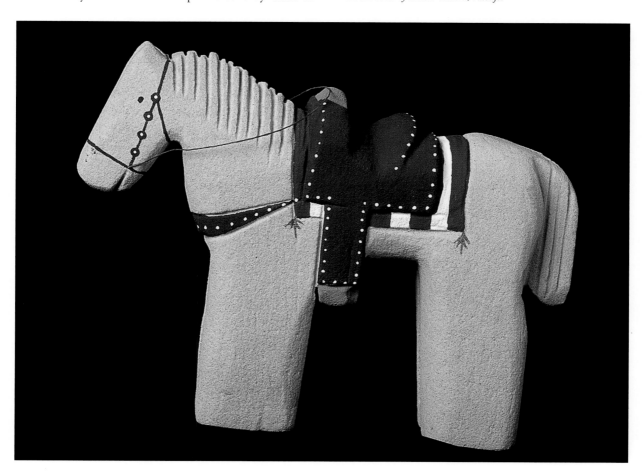

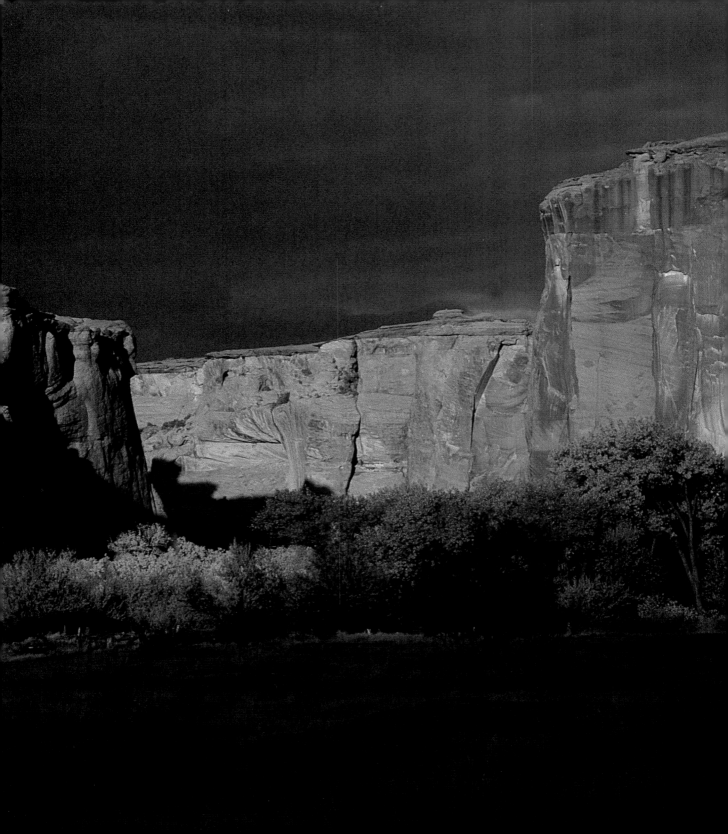

ʃ

WEAVING

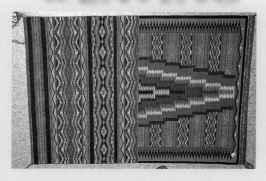

Combination of Burntwater and Wide Ruins weaving designs by Emma Roan, Navajo.

AMONG THE MORE IMPORTANT and revered deities in the pantheons of the Southwestern tribes—particularly the Pueblo peoples (including Hopis) and the Navajos—is a goddess figure known as Spider Woman or Spider Grandmother. In numerous stories of the creation, she is credited, in one way or another, with spinning the world into existence and, whenever needed, extricating the People from grievous troubles. Like the Greek Athena, she is wise and, of course, a weaver. Among many other matters in which she provided crucial instruction, she taught the People to weave.

Many of the Rio Grande tribes and other Pueblo communities weave, but the Navajos have deservedly gained a worldwide reputation as the preeminent master weavers. A Navajo woman clad in turquoise and velvet, kneeling before her upright loom, is virtually the unofficial logo of the Navajo people. The most frequently encountered pieces for sale are traditional sashes, which are instantly recognizable from the luminous green and red patterns woven into the black background.

The Hopi weave almost entirely for their own purposes. The men do the weaving—of wedding robes and shrouds. A groom-to-be's uncles are responsible for weaving the bride's wedding robes from white cotton (they formerly used a variety of wild cotton but now use the cultivated kind). These robes have red and black designs on the ends and fringes, each design with a highly symbolic meaning.

A Hopi wedding ceremony cannot take place until the robes are complete. In addition, the Hopi bride clad in her wedding robe must also carry, rolled up in a reed "suitcase," a mirror-image robe that will serve as her shroud and will carry her to the land of the spirits at the appropriate time. A further complication: if the union produces a female child prior to the ceremony, she too must have a white robe, postponing the ceremony again.

NAVAJO RUGS

In old tradition and practice, Navajo weavers produced blankets—worn against the bitter winters that strike the northern parts of the Southwest—and saddle blankets. Weaving with wool came, of course, with the arrival of the long-haired Spanish sheep called *churro,* and through Pueblo influence in the seventeenth century.

At some point, the Navajos began to produce what are called "chief blankets"—red, white, blue, and black blankets. The Navajos, like all Apacheans, didn't have what could be thought of as "chiefs." According to Tom Baker of the Tanner Chaney Gallery in Albuquerque, chief blankets were made for the chiefs of Plains tribes and traded for the metal (at that time, copper) fasteners of Plains buckskin leggings, which Navajos, with their usual inventiveness and a little influence from Mexicans, soon used to make concha belts.

The history of Navajo weaving thereafter is a continuous and complex story of multiple materials, styles, and influences, both artistic and commercial. The most significant influence, perhaps, was the arrival in the late nineteenth century of white traders who established trading posts in various parts of the reservation and served as powerful links between the Navajos and the outside world and its cash economy.

At first, as markets for traditional Navajo blankets dried up, the traders offered new designs and bought rugs by the pound. Quality declined. Then some astute traders such as Lorenzo Hubbell at Ganado, Arizona, and J. B. Moore at Crystal, New Mexico, began rewarding weavers for higher quality work. Throughout the vast Navajo Reservation, in locales like Crystal and Two Grey Hills, these men helped Navajo weavers create distinctive local styles that appealed to both the Navajo sense of design and meaning and to the public.

There are innumerable stories about the source of this design richness. The *storm pattern* rug is said by some (and denied by others) to have derived from a turn-of-the-twentieth-century design on a flour sack. Be that as it may, the storm pattern embodies a fundamental concept of the Navajo view of the world. Medicine man Andy Tonobah holds that several of the geometric subpatterns

Storm Pattern rug by Tina Conn, Navajo.

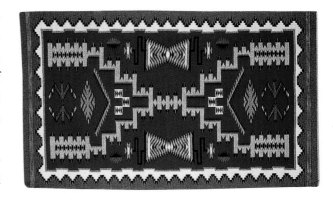

THE NAVAJOS

Referring to themselves as the Diné (pronounced dee-NEH and meaning "the people"), the Navajos are by far the largest Southwestern tribe at about 220,000, and they inhabit a reservation the size of West Virginia that lies in northeastern Arizona and northwestern New Mexico as well as a small portion of southern Utah—in all, more than 17 million acres. They now proclaim themselves the Navajo Nation and have made their capital Window Rock, Arizona. As their numbers alone would suggest, they are among the most resilient and adaptable tribal people in North America.

When they arrived in the northwestern region of present-day New Mexico sometime before A.D. 1500, they were typical of the Athapaskan migrants, living in extended family groups that could associate into larger bands as needed, hunting and gathering, and practicing a certain amount of horticulture. Like the other Apacheans, they engaged in raiding forays, particularly on the Pueblo people, and were raided in return. This activity increased in intensity with the arrival of the Spanish, who referred to these people as the "Apaches de Navajo," a name derived from a Jemez word meaning either "fields in a wide arroyo" or perhaps "take from fields."

The Navajos took part in the Pueblo Revolt of 1680, and they provided a haven for a number of Pueblo people chiefly from Jemez who had fled their traditional homes. These Pueblo immigrants brought to the Navajos a variety of cultural traits, from multicolored pottery styles to masked dancers performing in plazas and an elaborate system of clans, and there was a good deal of intermarriage as well as cultural absorption. Stone houses were added to, but never replaced, the traditional Navajo hogan (pronounced HOE-gahn), typically an eight-sided house made of mud spread over log supports, which served as a dwelling and also a place for ceremonial purposes.

Within some fifty years, the Navajos shed some of this new culture—the stone *pueblitos* and the elaborate plaza dances, for example—and returned to their more shamanistic ceremonies, but these had been greatly enriched by the addition of sandpainting and other practices. Many hold that during this period of cultural absorption and transformation, the Apaches de Navajo became truly the distinct culture of the Navajos.

By the mid-eighteenth century, the Navajos had also taken up the raising of Spanish sheep with great gusto and had become a chiefly pastoral society, though still practicing a limited horticulture and supplementing all this with hunting—and raiding. By the time the U.S. government took over the territory in 1848, the Navajos were major contributors to the great turmoil of the region, and after several years and various attempts to make treaties, the government decided to remove them and sent an expedition under Colonel Kit Carson to do so. Navajos were rounded up, their fields burned and sheep slaughtered, and in 1864 some 8,000 were marched to a camp in eastern New Mexico called Bosque Redondo. This was the Long Walk. They suffered from many of the ills associated with concentration camps everywhere.

Four years later, their numbers greatly reduced, they were allowed to return north to a large reservation encompassing land on both sides of the present Arizona–New Mexico border, where they resumed their old ways and rapidly expanded territorially, mostly to the west and the south.

Traditional cultural life has flourished up to today, centered around elaborate healing ceremonies conducted by medicine men for a variety of purposes. The ceremony is often a four- to nine-day ritual involving an intricate sandpainting that is created on the floor of a hogan and on which the patient sits. The medicine man's chants (which recapitulate long segments of the Navajo creation stories) also serve to bring into action certain spiritual essences called the Holy People, or Yei-be-cheis, who cleanse the patient. Another ceremonial feature central to Navajo (and Apache) life is a girl's coming-of-age, a four-day ritual in which she becomes a woman, with all that implies in a matrilineal and, to a degree, matriarchal society.

Today, many Navajos live a traditional life in remote camps dotted here and there around the landscape; these consist of the households of an extended family, with houses of modern construction, hogans, shade houses (made of branches), and corrals for horses and, importantly, sheep, which remain economically and culturally a central part of Navajo life. At the same time, many Navajos (some with professional degrees) live in a few "urbanized" areas on the reservation, such as Window Rock, Fort Defiance, Chinle, and Kayenta, where they pursue livings in a variety of jobs ranging from tribal government, teaching, and health-care positions to small businesses—in retail, tourism, and even manufacturing. The tribe derives a considerable portion of its annual budget from the leasing of mineral rights on the reservation—in particular, coal. The Navajos still count on federal assistance in such realms as education and health care. In addition, countless Navajos make a living, or supplement their income, from the production of crafts.

In recent years, the tribal government has reorganized itself into three distinct branches—judicial, executive (led by a president), and legislative (a large tribal council, which handles all secular affairs within the tribe and relations with outside entities, from industry to county, state, and federal government departments).

You will see more work by Navajo artists in the chapters on pottery, basketry, and jewelry.

found in rugs mimic the designs that emerge in the complex form of the string game (like cat's cradle) Navajos play, and that these games are intended in part to teach children the shapes of the seven major constellations in the night sky. In any event, there is nothing arbitrary about the pattern of any Navajo rug.

At the turn of the past century, there was a great deal of experimentation with aniline dyes and the use of pre-dyed wool with a nearly gaudy array of colors. Both were used in the so-called "Germantown" rugs. Some of the rugs of this period were referred to pejoratively as "eyedazzlers." At the urging of people like Mary Cabot Wheelwright (founder of the Wheelwright Museum of the American Indian in Santa Fe), weavers in the 1920s began to return to traditional dyes, creating what is now called the Revival Period.

Today we find a plethora of distinctive patterns, color combinations, emphases, and styles.

At the turn of the twentieth century, the depiction of *yeis,* the Navajo Holy People, was incorporated into design motifs, but some of the medicine men objected on religious grounds. However, a medicine man in the late 1920s made rugs depicting actual sandpaintings used in ceremonies. Weavers make them today, but with an important detail left out or altered. They sometimes charge more for such a rug since they may have to pay for a healing ceremony for themselves for having made it.

Beyond the distinctive patterns of the traditional rugs, many weavers have taken to making "pictorials" such as the popular Tree of Life—which is full of birds—and scenes of trading posts and Navajo camps. Images from

life have been added, such as trains, airplanes, and virtually any other object that catches the weaver's eye and imagination. These are sometimes called "specialty rugs."

In the separate Navajo reservation near Zuni called Ramah, the local weavers have begun a cooperative to produce Navajo rugs in their own styles. They use wool from *churro* sheep that had fallen out of favor long ago but were bred back with the help of researchers at Utah State University. These weavers adhere to the old and time-consuming ways, and some rugs are adorned with the long hairs of the *churro.* Various traders have advised the Ramah cooperative that the hair is not appealing to most buyers as they observe the crispness of the stitches—another example of the continuing balancing act between tradition and the marketplace that confronts all traditional artisans.

Whatever the style, however, it is next to impossible to find a Navajo weaver who uses anything but the

Ganado Red by Desbah Evans, Navajo.

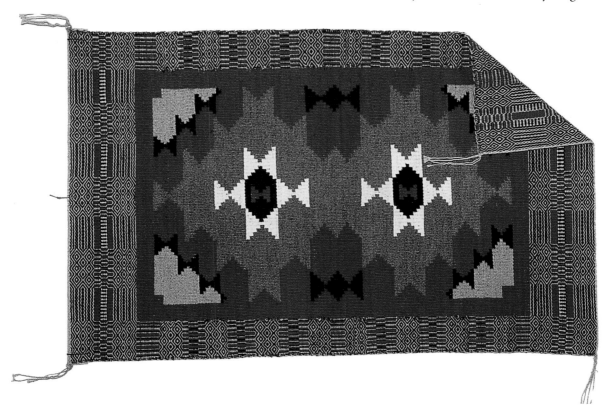

traditional upright loom, shown in the drawing below. It is believed in some parts of Navajoland that it was Spider Grandmother's husband who showed the Navajo men how to build looms for their wives. To this day it is considered proper for a man—a son-in-law, say—to make the ancillary tools, such as the wooden comb-like instrument the weaver uses to pack down the few inches of weft as she proceeds.

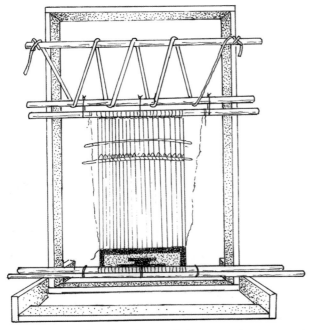

A weaver has the choice of shearing, cleaning, and spinning the wool herself from her own sheep, having it commercially cleaned and prepared, or using one-ply or four-ply commercial wool. She may use vegetal or aniline dyes. All these decisions are the weaver's to make and do not typically affect the value of the final product.

BUYING NAVAJO RUGS

Navajo rugs can seem expensive, with some fetching more than $10,000. One reason for the cost can be found in the table below, compiled at Wide Ruins Trading Post (in Arizona) and posted in Garland's Navajo Rugs in Sedona, Arizona. In 1973 a weaver was timed as she went through the entire procedure of producing a 3 x 5-foot vegetal-dyed rug.

ACTIVITY	HOURS
Shearing (2 sheep)	2
Cleaning the wool	10
Carding	40
Spinning	90
Washing	8
Native plant gathering	4
Dyeing	40
Loom construction	16
Warping the loom	18
Weaving	160
TOTAL	388

Assuming the weaver had no other chores to accomplish and worked only a regular eight-hour day, five-day week, this adds up to nearly two and a half months. A thousand dollars, say, for such an effort can hardly be thought of as exorbitant.

A main factor in the price of a Navajo rug is obviously its size. Other factors are:

1. **Tightness.** The finer the wool and therefore the more lines per inch, the more valuable the rug.
2. **Complexity of design.** The more complex the design, the more expensive the rug.
3. **Color changes.** An aspect of overall complexity, this has to do with the number of color changes per line of weft.
4. **The artist.** Some weavers have achieved a specific reputation for excellence, and this adds to the price.

A perfect Navajo rug is a rarity, as Bill Malone, a trader and authority on Navajo weaving, points out. Even the greatest weavers sometimes make a mistake. "A lot of

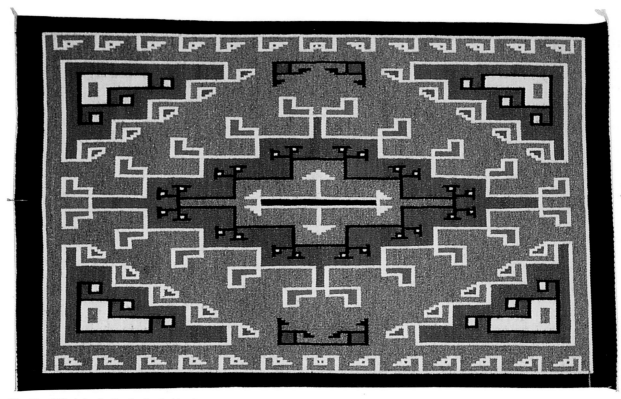

Two Grey Hills design by Carolyn Lewis, Navajo.

people are looking for the perfect rug at the lowest possible price. But we buy rugs from little old ladies who don't see quite so well anymore, and young girls just starting out. So some rugs may have slightly uneven edges, or color variations, or other little errors. You have to do that to keep the craft going."

FAKES

There is a long tradition, especially in Mexico, of making copies of Navajo rugs, and these have sometimes been palmed off as the real thing. There are several ways to tell the difference, and many of these have been set forth in detail in Noël Bennett's booklet, *Genuine Navajo Rug: How to Tell,* produced for the Indian Arts and Crafts Association.

- Mexican rugs (but even some Navajo rugs) are made from commercially scoured and spun yarns that lack the wool's natural lanolin, and henceforth aren't as strong, have no residual smell of sheep, and are lighter in weight.

- Mexican rugs are made from commercially dyed yarns, and thus there will be no color variation within an area of one hue. (The same applies to some Navajo rugs.) Navajo reds tend to be deeper, the grays more irregular (being made of black and white mixed, while Mexican grays are completely uniform and unsubtle).

- Mexican and Hispanic American looms are horizontal while Navajo looms are vertical. The vertical loom puts a greater tension on the warp (the up-and-down strings), and this, plus the weaver having regularly packed down

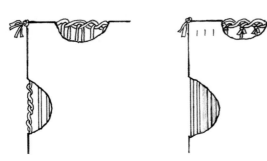

In Navajo rugs (left), the outer warp string is usually wrapped with the sel-vage cord, creating a four-strand knot in the corners. The warp is not bunched at the edge. Along the top, the warps are continuous. In Mexican imitations (right), there may be several warp clusters at the edge, and no sel-vage cord. The warps are knotted top and bottom and woven back into the rug, making a ridged end.

small areas with a comb-like fork, results in a rug that is densely packed and stiff, with no warp showing. Mexi-can imitations are less well packed, each line of weft being beaten down all at once with a horizontal beater.

• Thanks to the vertical loom, the outer lines of warp are tight. A Navajo rug will never (except for a few saddle blankets) have bunched warps. But in a Mexican rug, with its looser warp, the outer warp strings will typically be bunched together in a group of two or three lines to help make the edge straight.

Old Style rug by Mary Lee Begay, Navajo.

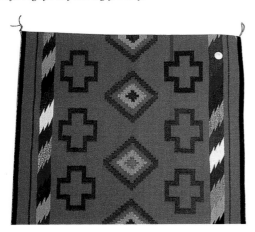

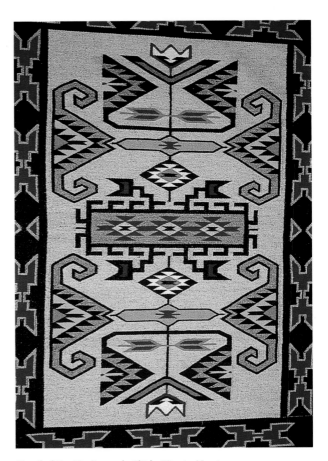

Detail of Teec Nos Pos rug by Shirley Tsinnie, Navajo.

In addition, a Navajo weaver may include a side sel-vage cord along with the outermost string of warp; the Mexicans do not do this.

• Mexican rugs are woven several to one stringing of the loom and then cut off, leaving strands of warp at either end as a kind of fringe. These used to be left dangling, but now imitators are knotting them and weaving them back into the ends of the rug, leaving a ridged texture along the bottom and top that you can feel with your fin-gers. Navajo weavers warp their looms for each rug, and use the entire warp, thus leaving no fringe and no ridge.

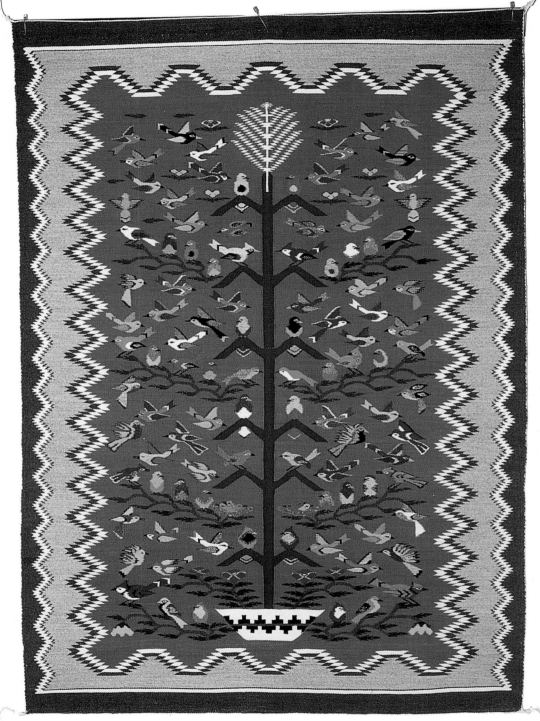

Tree of Life by Evelyn Tsosie, Navajo.

$\int$

CARVINGS

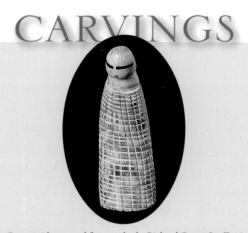

Corn maiden carved from antler by Richard Quam Jr., Zuni.

THROUGHOUT TIME AND THE WORLD, those with the urge and the knack to shape three-dimensional objects have used virtually every available natural material—bone, stone, wood—and the native peoples of the American Southwest are no exception. Carvers are to be found in virtually any Southwest tribe.

The carver's talent is, of course, very often a part of jewelry making, and the line between what might be called a carved fetish and jewelry is a blurry one. A carved talisman worn on a thong or among beads around the neck or as part of an earring is both.

This section is chiefly concerned with two major genres or traditions of carvings—Zuni fetishes and Hopi katsina dolls. These are the most popular carvings of the region among collectors, the most commonly encountered, and in many ways the most deeply rooted in the cultures from which they spring.

ZUNI CARVINGS

These are often referred to as "fetishes," and some Zuni carvings that are sold are indeed in the form of traditional and sacred Zuni fetishes. But actual fetishes require a

THE ZUNIS (PRONOUNCED ZOO-NEEZ)

The Zunis call themselves *Shiwi,* and archaeologically their origins remain mysterious. People who presumably are ancestral lived in the same area, centered some thirty miles south of today's Gallup, New Mexico, at least as early as A.D. 700, and showed cultural traits derived or taken from both Anasazi and Mogollon culture areas as the centuries passed. The Zuni language is unrelated to any other, though evidence exists linking it to a now extinct Californian tongue.

The Spanish first glimpsed Zuni in 1539, having come upon the quite elaborate village of Hawikuh (now a ruin some ten miles southwest of the present town of Zuni). The village fed the Spanish fantasy about the "seven cities of gold." A year later, Coronado arrived and subdued the Indians violently, finding neither gold nor other riches. Up until this time, the Zunis practiced agriculture similar to that of other Pueblo peoples, growing corn, squash, melons, and beans, and hunted game in the Zuni Mountains to the east. Relations with the Spanish (mostly friars) continued, alternating between acceptance and violent repulse, until the Pueblo Revolt of 1680, in which the Zunis participated wholeheartedly.

By 1692, they had abandoned all their previous settlements, concentrating in the present village of Zuni. Afterward they began to farm more far-flung fields and raise cattle, creating summer settlements that later became permanent, such as Ojo Caliente. In addition to a continuing love-hate relationship with Catholicism, the Spanish brought livestock, certain crops such as wheat and orchard fruits, and a form of secular political governance that was added to the indigenous Zuni theocratic tradition.

In this tradition, control of Zuni affairs was in the hands of several priests aided by members of various societies such as the Bow clan. Every Zuni is born into the mother's clan (and is a child of the father's clan). This membership generally controls one's place in society and which of the several religious orders one may belong to, and these in turn define one's role in society. Some of these religious orders are geared to healing and curing, others to more esoteric and magical rites—some quite fearsome.

The Zuni masked dancers have much in common with those of the Hopi. But Zuni katsina dances, in addition to having a highly spiritual and rainmaking function, also were highly developed as social entertainment, even with a role in courtship, and were perceived as such. Perhaps most notable of all the Zuni katsinas are the Shalakos, enormously tall figures who, on a night in December, arrive in the village and bless new homes, among other things.

Secular leadership—now in the form of a democratically elected tribal council—has replaced priests in many matters and handles all relations with outside entities from the federal government on down. Today, the Zuni reservation is some 409,000 acres, and the tribe's population is about 10,000, making it one of the largest among the Pueblos. Most Zunis are bilingual in Zuni and English, although the original language is dwindling among youth. Most Zunis are actively engaged in the cash economy, even while maintaining much of the traditional religious and ceremonial life that was linked to the agricultural cycle.

A major economic activity is the making of jewelry and carved objects for sale, and there is a resurgence of pottery making; almost every Zuni family is engaged in crafts. Other sources of income are livestock, off-reservation jobs, employment with the tribal government, and in education on the reservation.

With all this acceptance of many aspects of modernity, the traditional ceremonial life and worldview remain strong. A beautiful example of the coexistence of Catholicism and traditional religion is at the Old Mission church, where Zuni artist Alex Seowtewa and his sons have painted the walls with a life-size panoply of Zuni katsinas. The Zuni worldview is based on a highly ordered universe, a spiritual geography that is both symbolic and real, based on the four cardinal directions and two others (up and down). Religious acts, great and small, are designed to make things right, to make participants "valuable" and "protected." This notion of making things right, of a kind of perfection, is carried over into many activities, including craftsmanship, where every craftperson's work is widely scrutinized for excellence.

You will see more work by Zuni artists in the chapters on pottery and jewelry.

blessing by a priest and are too sacred to be sold. Beyond traditional forms, the carvers make an astounding array of figures, both animal and human, and even the simplest Zuni animal carving looks very alive.

In the earliest period of the Zunis, the animals that charmed their prey into being caught with their breath and hearts were told they had to assist the people rather than do them harm. At some later time a deity set up six animals as the guardians of the six regions or directions. In addition to providing protection, the six animals served as messengers to and from the spirit world.

The animals and the directions were also associated with colors, as follows:

NORTH	MOUNTAIN LION	YELLOW
WEST	BEAR	BLUE
SOUTH	BADGER	RED
EAST	WOLF	WHITE
ABOVE	EAGLE	MULTICOLOR
BELOW	MOLE	BLACK

Stone representations of these sacred animals dating back to at least the seventh century have been found in the region the Zunis now inhabit, and no doubt they were used much as they are today—carried or worn for protection from harm and to assure success. The fetishes are believed to contain the spirit of the animal represented, and therefore the Zunis tie offerings of beads and tiny arrowheads on them with thread or string as well as provide them with cornmeal and water at winter solstice.

Crystal frog, artist unknown, Zuni.

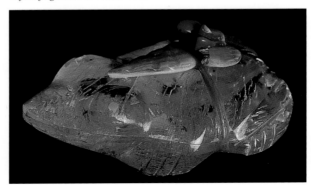

A second realm of animal protectors is associated with the hunt. They are the same as the six directional animals except that the coyote is to the west instead of the bear, and the wildcat replaces the badger in the south. Zuni men carry them to ensure a successful hunt.

The addition of a *heartline*—usually a crooked, lightning-like line that goes from the mouth of a fetish to its heart-lung area and ends with an arrow point—appears to be a recent (perhaps nineteenth-century) innovation, and is now common. It may be etched into the sides of

the fetish or inlaid with another material, such as turquoise or coral. Eyes are often inlaid as well.

The traditional fetish is not unlike those from earlier times, where the animal is minimally defined as if its form were already present in the stone. Legs are deemphasized, almost nonexistent. In earlier times, fetishes were made from locally available stone and sometimes painted the appropriate color. The most valuable fetish for the Zunis was a piece of stone that was found with the suggestive shape of an animal already present and thus needing little or no carving. It is this simplicity of shape that is emulated

Traditional mole by the Sheche family, Zuni.

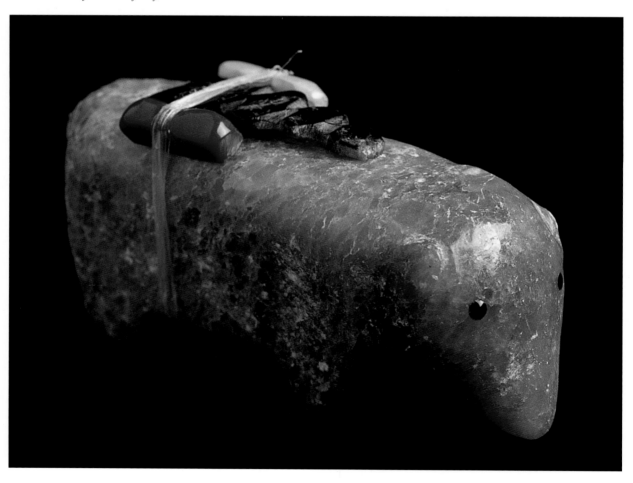

by carvers of traditional fetishes. As a result the animal shapes can all look bafflingly alike.

In general, identifying details are as follows:

MOUNTAIN LION TAIL UP AND ALONG THE BACK

BEAR NO TAIL OR STUBBY TAIL, SMALL ROUNDED EARS

BADGER FLATTENED BODY

WOLF NO TAIL, OR HANGING TAIL AND ERECT EARS

EAGLE BIRDLIKE IN FORM

MOLE SOMEWHAT POINTY NOSE, DOWN-POINTING

COYOTE LIKE WOLF BUT WITH TAIL STRAIGHT OUT, LESS BUSHY

WILDCAT THINNER, SHORTER TAIL AND MORE UPRIGHT EARS THAN COYOTE

Zunis make it very clear that fetishes carved for sale do not bear any particular religious significance and should be thought of as "carvings" rather than technically as fetishes. They have no objection to collectors' investing them with whatever religious significance they see fit. Zuni carvers have long produced other animal (and human) representations besides the directional and hunters' arrays, and some of these have more significance culturally than others. Before 1900, lynx, horse, ram, and turkey figures were collected by Smithsonian anthropologists. Since then, and particularly since the 1980s, when collecting Zuni carvings became highly popular, there has been a proliferation of subjects and of material. In addition to local stone such as serpentine and chert, carvers have used turquoise, pipestone, jet, fluorite, alabaster, amber, lapis, fossil ivory, and malachite, among other materials.

In whatever material, one finds carvings in varying amounts of realistic detail, from little to astonishingly precise, representing a host of subjects—lizards, fish, dinosaurs, skunks, dogs, frogs, deer, snakes, and so on. Of all of these, probably the most popular and the most often produced is the bear. Among the most distinctive of bear fetish designs is the long-necked, gracefully alert classic bear of the Quandelacy family.

Ancient fetishes were carved by scraping them with a sharp, hard stone, and smoothing them with a duller one. The arrival of modern lapidary equipment in the twentieth century has helped expand the use of exotic materials and new subjects and designs. This has permitted the Zuni fascination with miniaturization to flourish, with some pieces only an inch or so long bearing astoundingly intricate detailing. It is a rare Zuni household in which someone does not make fetishes, and it has been estimated that along with other crafts, they represent up to half of the personal income of the Zunis.

FETISH NECKLACES

In addition to the traditional type of fetish, which typically ranges from an inch and a half to five inches in length, are numerous smaller ones made for stringing on necklaces along with various kinds of heishi beads. These necklaces may have one kind of fetish—birds or bears, for example—all in one color or type of stone, or many different kinds of creatures. They may have one string or many. Read more about fetish necklaces in the "Jewelry" chapter.

HOPI KATSINA DOLLS

Perhaps the first thing to keep in mind is the distinction between a katsina and a katsina *doll*. The katsinas are a great panoply of ancestral, nature, and other spirits that, during approximately half the year, appear (as dancers) in the villages during ceremonies either in the kivas (underground chambers) or in the plazas. Katsina dolls, on the other hand, have always been first and foremost toys, not

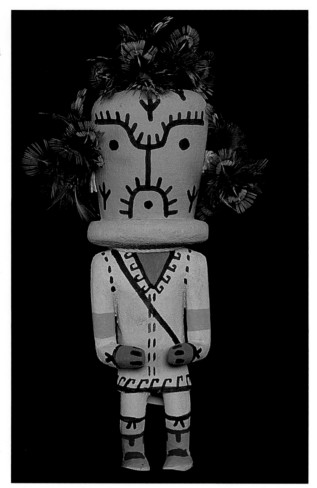

Sikyaqoqlo katsina doll, old-style carving by Clark Tenakhongva, Hopi.

In early times and today, the katsina spirits give dolls out to uninitiated girls during plaza dances (bows and arrows go to the boys). Typically a girl's first doll is a simple, flat doll (sometimes called a cradle doll) representing Hahay'iwuti, the mother of the katsinas, the gift being a prayer or wish that the girl will one day be fruitful. As the girl grows older, the katsinas give her dolls that are more and more three-dimensional.

In the latter part of the twentieth century, it became the practice to hang such gifts carefully on the wall to preserve them, rather than let them get worn out in the rough-and-tumble of play.

A second thing to be mindful of is that, for every generalization one may make about the katsinas and their representations as dolls, there are a host of exceptions. These arise for several reasons, of which the most important is that every Hopi—each is a member of one of thirty Hopi clans and a resident of one of twelve separate villages—may have a slightly different view of such things. There are some 400 katsinas at Hopi, and many who no longer appear but are remembered. There are, as well, hundreds of carvers, including, recently, a few women.

The earliest wood katsina dolls are surely lost to time, but examples of the flat kind with a simple break between head and body have been found dating back to the early 1700s. They have always been carved from the light, dry roots of the cottonwood tree. In early times they were carved in simple forms from one piece of root and colored with mineral and vegetal pigments. Later the Hopis took to making somewhat more realistic dolls, gluing on or pegging carved arms, legs, and other features. Many modern carvers have experimented with other woods such as balsa, but most have given them up in disgust. Today many methods are used, one of which is to create

religious idols. They are representations, but not representatives, of the katsinas.

According to Hopi linguist Emory Sekaquaptewa, their chief function was to be played with, and so they would eventually break or wear out and be discarded. As a boy in the 1930s, as he watched the men carving dolls in the kiva, they would occasionally send him out to the dump to see if he could find a cast-off but serviceable part, such as an ear, to be affixed to a new carving.

elaborate and detailed sculptures from a single, often branched, piece of wood.

Older, more sculptural dolls were cylindrical (like the root), with rudimentary arms and legs, the arms running down the sides and meeting in front. The Hopi sometimes refer to these as "stomachache dolls." In early times, the dolls were primed with a thin coat of white clay before being painted. Paints were made from iron oxide, copper ore, and colored clay. Tempera and poster paints

Cradle doll carved by Phillip Coochyamtewa, Hopi.

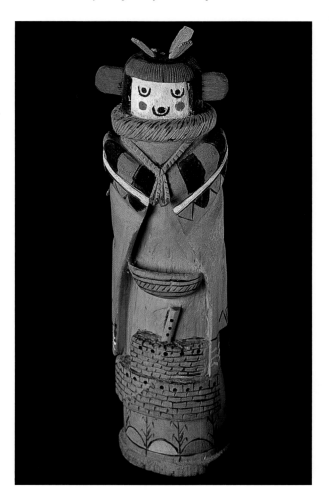

began to be used in the early twentieth century, and more recently, acrylics. New materials have also found wide use—for example, green yarn for the evergreen ruff that a katsina has around its neck. The use of feathers from migratory and songbirds (and all endangered or threatened birds) has been largely embargoed by federal wildlife laws, so carvers may use turkey and starling feathers that are sometimes dyed. Others get around the issue by carving the feathers out of wood.

James Barajas, buyer of katsina dolls for Phoenix's Heard Museum Shop, points out that older dolls made with the feathers of migratory birds and endangered birds may no longer be sold *by anyone.* Even those found in an estate collection and made long ago can only be donated to a museum or other legitimate research collection.

From about World War II, carvers began making dolls that show more action, with more precise rendering of proportion and musculature. This coincided with a rising interest in collecting katsina dolls and in making them for sale. Many of today's carvers pay great attention to the minutest detail such as the intricate designs on sashes. Some carvers dress their dolls with suede and leather, while others carve the clothing onto the doll. Today it is common for the carver to sign his work, typically on the bottom of the base.

Two major new styles have arisen recently. The first is highly sculptural, using the shape of the wood—its twists and turns—as an element of the doll's form. These are sculptures in the truest sense, often combining realism with abstraction, representing a katsina spirit rather than the spirit's embodiment in a dancer. However abstract such a piece may be, the face is always precise. Faces are usually very finely carved and detailed, and often much if not all of the wood is left unpainted, though perhaps stained.

THE HOPI (PRONOUNCED HOE-PEE)

The Hopi are the most remote and isolated of all the Pueblo tribes (they do not use the word "Pueblo" for themselves). For about a millennium they have lived in compact villages on three southern fingers of a huge landform called Black Mesa that is in the approximate center of the current Navajo reservation in northeastern Arizona. In all, some 7,300 Hopis live in twelve Hopi villages located (from east to west) on First, Second, and Third Mesa, with one outlying village (Moenkopi) some fifty miles to the west. The Third Mesa village of Oraibi vies with Acoma and Taos as among the oldest continuously inhabited places in the United States, having been settled about one thousand years ago.

The Hopi villages—with homes built mostly of local sandstone (not adobe, as in the New Mexico pueblos) and clustered tightly around plazas, with several kivas in each village—have traditionally been sovereign units in many respects. Like the highly independent, sometimes fractious, Greek city-states, they are tied together into a tribal unit by a common language and culture. Each mesa and its villages speaks a slightly different (though mutually understandable) dialect and has somewhat different traditions in such things as crafts. Since the 1930s, the villages have also been more closely knit by a tribal council with representatives from all of them; the council is responsible for certain internal secular affairs and for dealing with governments and other elements of the outside world.

A Hopi person is born into the mother's clan. There are some thirty clans, and clan membership is the glue that makes the Hopi one people. Each clan has an important social and ceremonial role—from spiritual leadership to the collection of sacred tobacco for ceremonial purposes—and each of these functions is needed and honored by all other Hopi.

Hopi history states that the clans arrived at the present location after passing through three previous worlds and after long subsequent migrations. The first to arrive, the Bear clan, according to prophecy stopped at the current location when a star shone during the daytime—perhaps the supernova of 1054. Some clans appear to have come from the south, bringing a Mesoamerican influence, others from the north, east, and west. This is reflected in the Hopi language, a Uto-Aztecan tongue common to Shoshoneans and certain Mexican tribes. (Today virtually all Hopi speak English, and the tribe is laboring mightily to keep the original language alive among its youth.)

The Bear clan supplies each village's leader, the *kikmongwi,* who plays a spiritual and religious role. In this highly matrilineal society, the kikmongwi's wife also plays a crucial leadership role.

For a millennium here (and presumably in other locations before that) the Hopi have practiced a sophisticated form of dry farming, producing a wealth of corn, beans, squash, and melons. Their highly complex annual ceremonial cycle is centered on agriculture, its most famous aspect being the katsinas, who dance in the village kivas and then in the plazas from winter solstice into late July. (During the rest of the year, they reside high in San Francisco Peaks, the remnants of a great volcano about 100 miles away in Flagstaff.)

In addition to the dances of the katsina society, into which most ten-year-old children are initiated but in which only males are publicly active, another well-known ceremony is the Snake Dance, a rain dance in which priests dance with rattlesnakes and other snakes in their mouths. (Snake Dance ceremonies are now held in only two villages and are closed to the public.) There are also several secret priestly societies, membership in which marks a further step toward spiritual adulthood. Their rituals and even purposes are a closely guarded secret even among the Hopi.

The Hopi were among the first people the Spanish encountered after the Zunis, but their very remoteness kept Spanish influence at a minimum. For a long period they tolerated the presence of Spanish friars in their midst, and they took up various items of agriculture and (less so) craft, but they participated in the Pueblo Revolt of 1680 by killing the friars and burning the missions.

Soon members of other pueblos to the east sought refuge at Hopi, and a group of Tewa-speaking people were finally permitted to build a First Mesa village where they would act as sentinels. This is Hano, still a quite distinct Hopi-Tewa group only partially assimilated after 300 years.

A combination of deep-seated conservatism and geographic remoteness kept Hopi culture little changed throughout the centuries as Spanish rule gave way first to Mexican (in 1823) and then to American (in 1848). A major threat was raiding by Utes and, since 1500, by Navajos, who gradually moved into aboriginal Hopi territories; the raids led to extremely complex and tragic land disputes that today are not thoroughly resolved. The Hopi reservation consists of 1.5 million acres.

In modern times, most of the villages are served by electricity and communal wells (Walpi on First Mesa is a notable exception), and such modern items as pickup trucks and TV sets are common. Today most Hopi children are educated—through high school—on the reservation and an increasing number go on to higher levels.

The Hopi worldview is extremely complex, rich, and cerebral—layered with what European culture thinks of as symbolic meanings. Corn, for example, has innumerable meanings and associations beyond its physical existence as food. Hopi corn comes in numerous colors, and six of these represent the four cardinal directions and up and down. Each color and each cardinal direction also denotes the clans that migrated from that direction. An ear of corn is also a child—the same Hopi word means a spent corn husk and the physical remains of a human life that has ended. The designs one finds on Hopi craft objects have similarly rich connotations, bespeaking entire realms of historical experience and meanings of a moral and philosophical nature, all of which fit into an orderly universe of which the Hopi are a part.

You will see more work by Hopi artists in the chapters on pottery, basketry, and jewelry.

Almost as a protest against the elaboration of the modern katsina doll, some carvers have returned to the "stomachache" style, using faded colors to mimic age.

COLLECTING KATSINA DOLLS

As a result of all these innovations and changes, as well as the variety of katsinas represented and the innumerable opinions among individual Hopi, the array of katsina dolls available can be bewildering to all but the most expert. Some serious collectors specialize in one or another general type or in the work of a single carver. No one has ever amassed what could be called a complete collection. Perhaps the finest collection in both scope and quality was assembled by the late Arizona senator Barry Goldwater. He donated it to the Heard Museum, where it is sometimes displayed.

Many collectors focus their efforts on particular kinds of katsina dolls, such as representations of animal katsinas. Bears and badgers, for example, are traditionally

"Sun Clown," by Regina Naha, Hopi.

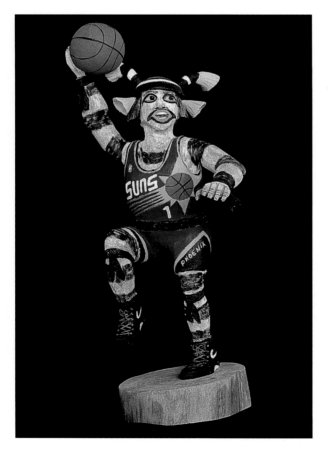

involved in healing. The eagle is a leader and a messenger to the next world. Ogres, James Barajas has found, are popular with businesspeople since, as disciplinarians, they stand for order and doing things properly.

Prices are dictated by excellence, the increasingly limited supply of cottonwood root, and size. They range widely—from about $150 to thousands of dollars for major works by well-known artists—but excellence and authenticity are to be found in all price ranges. The following points should be kept in mind.

Material. All Hopi katsina dolls are made of cottonwood root. Period. It is lightweight, unlike pine or cottonwood *branches,* for example, but solid, unlike balsa. There should be no cracks in the wood.

Painting. Except for those dolls that revive the older styles, lines and the edges of color areas should be precise and firm. The paint should not smudge with handling (most carvers use a spray fixative over the paint).

Carving. Detail is usually the key, the finer the better (except in revival styles). Proper proportion of body parts and also a sense of movement and elan are important in "action" dolls. Correct body proportions are more difficult for a carver to achieve than fine details.

Finishing. Sanding and otherwise finishing a doll is an important—and time-consuming—task. Prices can be higher for a doll that is more meticulously finished.

Costumery. Whether carved or made of other materials and added, it has to be present. Very few authentic dolls are empty-handed.

Identity. The doll itself should be identifiable as a particular katsina. A dealer should know, if the piece is not labeled, and there are a number of books that illustrate many of the available katsinas. In addition, the carver should sign the doll and identify his village.

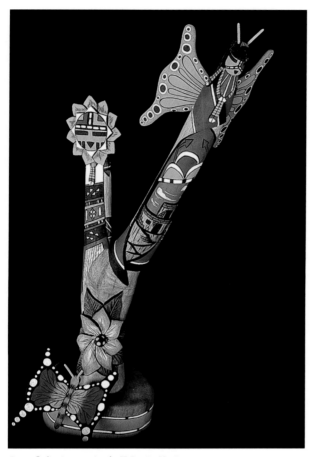

Butterfly katsina carving by T. Lewis, Hopi.

A new collector should feel confident if, having considered the points above, he or she finds a desirable katsina doll in an affordable price range. To a Hopi carver the most important aspect of a katsina doll is its faithfulness to the katsina, and this faithfulness can be achieved either simply or elaborately.

FAKES

The right material and the identity of the katsina spirit represented are the most important factors in avoiding fake katsina dolls. There is a considerable trade in them

and they are often made by other Indians or by foreigners. Some Navajos who make knockoff katsina dolls have recently been startled, even outraged, to discover that Mexicans have begun making Navajo-style katsinas and undercutting them in the market. Such imitations (to be kind) tend to have the wrong material and detail, and are often sloppily painted and ineptly carved. Navajo versions all tend to have the same kilt, James Barajas points out, whereas some five standard variations of kilts adorn the Hopi katsinas and therefore the dolls.

Reputable galleries and retailers do not carry imitations or fakes, and certainly don't represent them as Hopi. Even so, it is wise to be wary. A tip-off is a shelf of similarly shaped dolls all about the same height—they are probably mass-produced. The first question one should ask is, "Is it made by a Hopi carver?"

CATEGORIES OF KATSINAS AND KATSINA DOLLS

Any general categorization of katsina dolls is arguable, but the scheme of Barton Wright, a leading non-Hopi chronicler of katsina dolls, is a helpful way to look at this array of objects.

Chief katsinas. The word "chief" refers to importance, not to a political office. The chief katsinas are major figures, each associated with a particular clan or clans and, like the clans, each has a special function that benefits all the people. They are, in a sense, the elders of the katsinas. Among the more than fifty chief katsinas are:

Crow Mother, considered by many to be the mother of the katsinas, supervises the initiation of children into the katsina society. At the Bean Dance, she leads the other katsinas into the village, bearing kernels of corn and bean sprouts in a basket, signaling the beginning of the new agricultural season.

Eototo is the spiritual equivalent of the village *kik-mongwi,* or father (always a member of the Bear clan). He uniquely knows all the ceremonies. His simple appearance bespeaks his great age.

Masau'u is the deity who provided the Hopi with their land in this world, and he rules it and the underworld. He controls the passage of souls to the underworld and the emergence of the katsinas into the land of the living.

Guard katsinas. Often fierce- or angry-looking, and often carrying yucca whips and/or other weapons, these warriors or guards act something like policemen at various community and ceremonial functions. Some, like *Wuyak-kuita,* the Broad-Faced Katsina, have large, bulbous eyes.

Ogres. The ogres make their appearance in the First and Second Mesa Hopi villages in February and March. First an ogre woman *(So'yokwuuti)* arrives, warning that the ogres will soon appear demanding cooked food from girls, hunted food from boys. Later, ogres arrive, hooting and shattering the quiet, demanding the food and explaining that, if it is not to be had, they will put the children in their burden baskets instead and eat them later. In the course of this terror, the ogres explain loudly what each child, and sometimes each adult, has done wrong. Once the family delivers some food and promises that the children will be good, they can be wrested from the ogres' grasp. Afterward, everyone present is given a special blessing, and the ogres are forcibly driven out of the village.

Most of the ogre katsinas have long beaked mouths, and they often appear with disheveled hair and feathers. Some appear with knives, saws, and other scary implements.

Katsina women. There are female katsinas—mothers, wives, sisters—and they wear the traditional black dress called a *manta,* with a red and white blanket over the shoulders. Perhaps the most familiar are the *katsin-manas,*

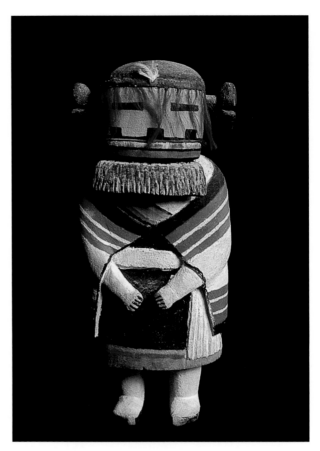

Katsin-mana, an old-style katsina maiden, artist unknown, Hopi.

who grind corn throughout the Home Dance in late July when the year's brides are introduced to the katsinas and to the cycle of life they will experience as matrons, ending in their death.

Clowns. There are several kinds of Hopi clowns, some katsinas, others not, and they play various roles in the Hopi ceremonies, most often in the summer plaza dances.

Mudheads (called *Koyemsi* in Hopi) are brown, dressed in kilts, and often carry rattles and other accoutrements. They have bulbous ears and topknots. Sometimes they are among the singers at a plaza dance; other times they challenge Hopis to footraces, or outsiders to a game or test of skill. Their faces completely covered, they are katsinas. They are also important messengers, carrying Hopi prayers to the rain gods and other supernaturals.

Koyaala are white clowns with black horizontal stripes on their bodies, black markings on their mouths and eyes, and two stalk-like appendages sticking up from their heads. Perhaps borrowed from the Tewa tradition of the Rio Grande pueblos (where they are called *Koshare),* they carry on at plaza dances with various kinds of amusing, exaggerated behavior. In other instances, the clowns are *Tsuku,* often painted yellow, mostly naked but for loincloths, and they typically appear in the plaza descending ladders backward from the surrounding roofs. They proceed to do everything backward, turning the Hopi Way on its head, going from bad behavior to worse, from peccadillo to real sin. They can be ribald, even gross, until they finally taunt and even try to imitate and join the katsinas. At this point they are attacked by whipper katsinas and soundly beaten until they promise to repent.

The Koyaala and Tsuku (the latter means "teach a lesson") will mock both Hopi fads and crazes, accuse Hopis in the audience of bad behavior, and intimidate outsiders.

Other katsinas. The large group of other katsinas are referred to as "mixed." In addition there are animal katsinas, many of which are healers and advisers; bird katsinas such as the Warrior Owl who reprimands the clowns; and those representing insects, plants, and other creatures of nature.

ZUNI KATSINA DOLLS

There are a few carvers at Zuni who produce dolls that are similar to those of the Hopi, but are representations of the Zuni katsina spirits. These are rarely encountered in galleries and usually labeled as Zuni. Often they have thin, square bases as opposed to the rounder section of cottonwood root used by the Hopis.

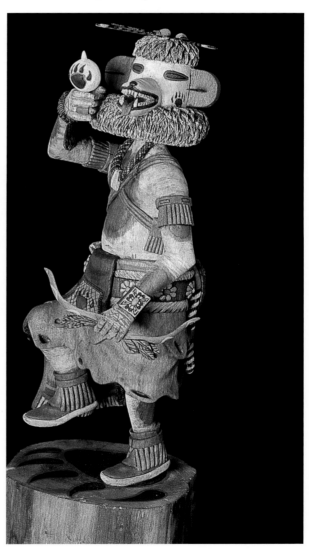

Kocha Honaw (White Bear Katsina), by Kevin Secakuku, Hopi.

CHAPTER FOUR

POTTERY

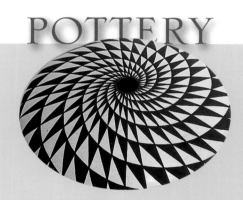

Seed pot by Dorothy Torivio, Acoma.

THROUGHOUT MUCH OF THE SOUTHWEST, the land underfoot is littered with shards, the remains of pots both ancient and recent, each bespeaking the hours it took an Indian woman to collect clay from some special place, prepare it, fashion it into a pleasing but utilitarian shape, fire it, use the product, and cast it aside when it broke. This procedure has been followed for more than 2,000 years, and hundreds of different styles have come and gone, with many revived and forgotten again. The process still goes on.

Introduced from Mexico between A.D. 100 and 200, the art of making pottery rapidly spread north and began to flower, particularly among the concentrated populations known today as the Anasazi and Mogollon peoples. Plain brown pottery gave way to decorated forms—black, white, and gray—and eventually various shades of red were added, making pots of more than two colors, or *polychrome*. While primarily utilitarian, all pottery had a spiritual component. It came directly from the earth and returned to the earth, and the earth was seen as a sacred,

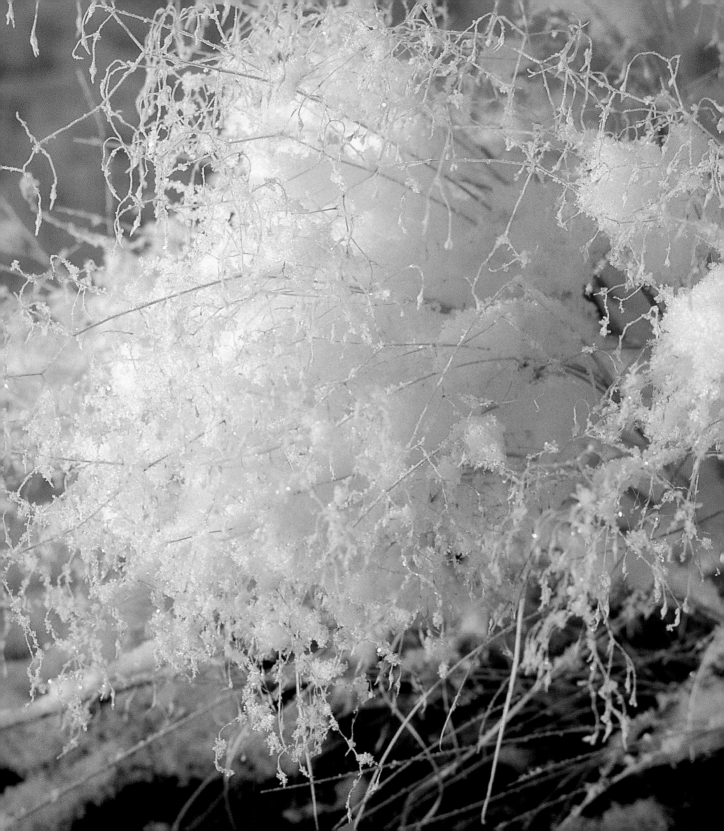

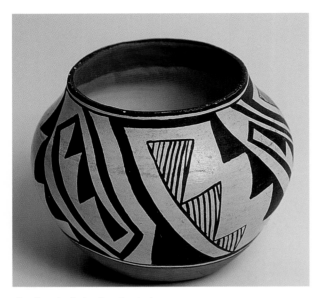

Small pot by the late Lucy Lewis, Acoma.

generative mother. Large *ollas* were used for storing dry foods and water, smaller ones for cooking. There were pitchers, mugs, and canteens, and bowls in various shapes and sizes were used for cooking and eating.

Throughout the centuries, pottery was frequently traded, and this commerce among the early peoples of the region no doubt sped the cross-fertilization and spread of new techniques and design systems.

In the late nineteenth century, manufactured ceramic and metal containers began to replace pottery in many Indian homes. As the need dwindled, so did the art. But at about this time, private and museum collectors began seeking out older pots. Then the growth of the tourist trade provided a different kind of market. For many years, much of what was made for sale amounted to curios. In the early part of the twentieth century, non-Indian and Indian organizations began to encourage the old craft, providing markets, competitions, prizes, and even research into old pottery traditions. The craft started to flourish again. Sales to collectors and to the growing tourist market became for many Indian people an important source of family income.

The revival of traditional styles and the invention of new ones became an important source of community identity and pride. In a number of instances in the twentieth century, and more and more often today, Indian potters have achieved the status of true artists, striking out into new territory, using new materials, techniques, and styles to create pottery that reflects an increasingly personal self-expression. Yet local traditions persist, not only in themselves, but as inspiration for even the most individualistic Indian artists. It is these traditional forms and techniques that the following section—organized tribe by tribe in alphabetical order—addresses. You will notice that most of these pottery makers are from the Pueblo tribes, although we also discuss pottery by Navajos.

HOW POTS ARE MADE

All local clay has its own special properties that determine what a potter can do with it, and over the centuries this has played an important role in local styles. But the basic technique for making pottery has always been the same—the *coil and scrape method.*

But first the clay must be collected—itself a laborious process—and prepared. It must be dried, then soaked and sieved to remove impurities and foreign matter like stones and roots. A *temper* is then added that promotes a uniform porosity, reducing shrinkage and cracking when the pot is dried and fired. The most common tempers are sand and powdered rock or old pottery shards (a nice bit of recycling). The clay is then set aside and kept damp—a process called *curing.*

The potter next collects a variety of vegetable and mineral matter to make paint. Vegetal paints tend to carbonize and turn black when fired; various kinds of ground-up rock yield a variety of hues at the red end of the spectrum.

From a flat base, the potter builds up a series of coils, or ropes, of clay. These are then smoothed and scraped into a uniform thickness with a curved tool. A potsherd will do, or a piece of gourd, as well as many modern implements.

Next, the potter may apply a *slip,* a thin liquid coat of clay, and, while the pot is still damp, polish it—often with a smooth stone. The next step is to paint decorations on the pot—traditionally a finely stripped yucca shoot has served as a paintbrush, and many of today's potters find this a better tool than the finest and most expensive artists' brushes.

Pot with fire-clouds, by Alice Cling, Navajo.

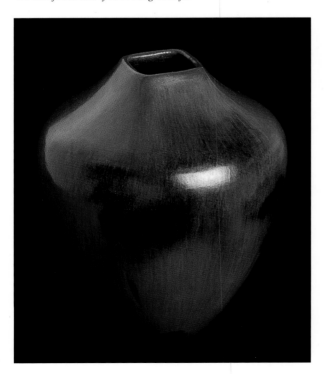

Some kinds of clay permit the pot to be sun-dried, but most pottery is fired. Today, some potters use electric kilns that offer greater control over the firing process, but firing is typically done outdoors. One or more pots will be surrounded with fuel—usually cow or sheep manure—which is then ignited. Any imperfections in a pot may now cause it to explode in the heat. If a piece of burning manure slips and hits the pot, it causes a dark smudge called a *fire-cloud.* Al Anthony—founder of Albuquerque's Adobe Gallery (which later closed and consolidated with Adobe Gallery, Santa Fe)—thinks fire-clouds are wonderful because they tell you immediately that the pot was fired in the traditional manner and not in a kiln. Some potters deliberately create fire-clouds for a specific depth of color. Once fired, and still warm, the pots are removed.

Some potters paint or etch designs on *greenware,* pottery that is made by pouring liquid clay into a mold—a method yielding pots that are identical and perhaps perfectly symmetrical. Al Anthony points out that greenware clay is a chalky, dead white, very smooth, and can have residual seams from the mold. Most potters will abrade the seams away on the outside of the pot, but many leave them on the inside where they can be felt. Greenware, Anthony says, is used most widely at Acoma and Laguna (whose traditional clay is white, but tinged with a very light brown, rather than being dead white).

BUYING POTS

As in anything else, when buying Indian pottery you should first and foremost be personally pleased with the appearance of the object. In judging a pot's excellence, a sophisticated collector will look for "balance"—how well the design fits the shape. Another important quality is clean brushwork in the designs.

However much a particular pot may be part of a tribal tradition, the individual potter is unique. Each puts as much of herself or himself into the pot as possible; the clay speaks to the potter, and the potter speaks to the world. For a buyer to "hear" this artistic conversation is a matter of experience and feel. There are no simple standards to rely on.

A buyer is entitled to a great deal of information. One should feel free to ask these basic questions of an individual, store, or gallery:

- **Who made it?** Many potters sign their work on the bottom and often give a tribal identification.
- **Was it made by the coil and scrape method?** (The value of greenware will not increase with time; it is at best "handcrafted" as opposed to "handmade," where *all* components were shaped by hand.)
- **Were natural, local clay and natural paints used?**
- **How was it fired?** Naturally (sheep manure at Hopi, cow manure in the other pueblos)? Or by kiln? Was it fired *after* the paints were applied?

Zuni pot, 1890s, artist unknown.

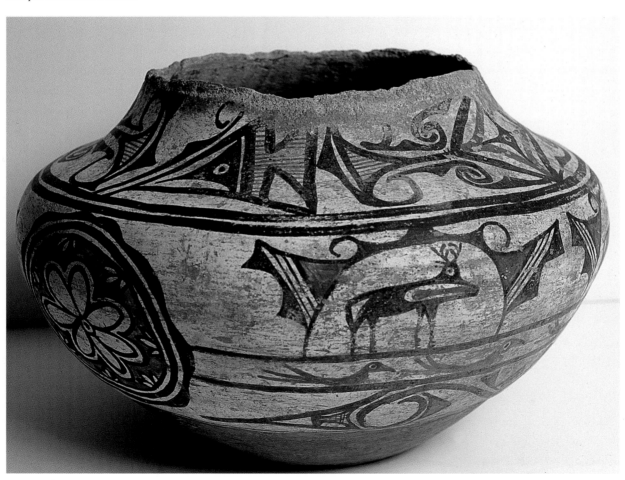

The price of pottery varies from a few tens of dollars to thousands, the high end paid for work of the most highly skilled and highly regarded potters. Old pots are extremely valuable. Note that an older pot will show signs of use and wear, even of repaired breaks. Such evidence is not a minus for the serious collector. If you don't like signs of wear, don't buy the pot. It is possible to restore some damage on many types of pots, but according to Al Anthony of Adobe Gallery, blackware and most polished redware *cannot* be restored satisfactorily; at best, restored blackware will "look like it was painted with automobile paint."

Many of the finest potters' work is represented in major galleries along with the work of less-known artisans. An excellent place to look for less expensive but totally creditable pots is in the various trading posts on the reservations, along with tribal craft stores and individual homes (which may have signs out front saying "Pottery for Sale"). Most trading posts feel obliged to buy the work of younger and less-experienced potters as well as the more accomplished to encourage a market that will keep the craft alive and well.

Generally speaking, the marked price reflects not only the time it took to create the object, but also the skill of the artist as measured by community and market standards. Prices can change from year to year and place to place, depending on a host of factors. As with any other arts or crafts, the best way to get a feel for the price of these objects is comparison shopping.

ACOMA POTTERY

Best known for intensely white (and white-slipped) ware with a matte finish and finely detailed black cross-hatching, interlocking scrolls, and repeated geometrical

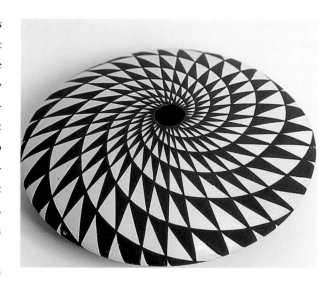

Seed pot by Dorothy Torivio. Acoma.

motifs, Acoma pottery often achieves M. C. Escher-like optical illusional patterns adapted to the shape of the vessel. Typically, Acoma pottery is extremely thin-walled—the thinnest in the Southwest.

Acoma pots are also seen with polychrome painting, particularly in designs from nature: a parrot-like bird, flowers, or Zuni-like deer with heartline (an arrow running from the mouth to the heart). Here a yellow slip is used that turns red, orange, or brown when fired. Bases are often dipped in slip to make red-orange.

The modern tradition resulted largely from the work of Lucy Lewis and Marie Chino, beginning in the 1950s, who introduced prehistoric—particularly Mimbres—design elements (lizards, fish, insects, and so forth) that continue to be popular today among Acoma potters.

Acoma clay, from a secret source, is hard-fired, making durable lightweight walls that ring if tapped. (Many modern potters use a commercial kiln; you should ask how the pot is fired.) The clay is usually ground and

ACOMA PUEBLO (PRONOUNCED ACK-A-MA)

One of New Mexico's nineteen Pueblo peoples, the Acoma tribe resides in its aboriginal location on a reservation of some 263,000 acres about an hour west of Albuquerque. The first European visitor, a Spaniard in 1540, described the site as "a very strange place built on solid rock." He referred to the main pueblo, *A-ku*, today sometimes called Sky City, located on a 400-foot fortress-like mesa. Along with Taos and the village of Oraibi in Hopi, Acoma is one of the oldest continuously inhabited places in the United States; people have lived in this pueblo looking out for miles over an awesome landscape of mesas, deep valleys, arroyos, and rolling hills for at least one thousand years.

Jug pot from the 1930s, artist unknown, Acoma.

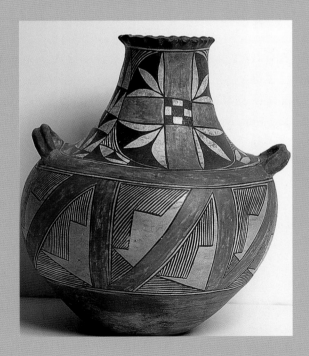

The language of Acoma is Keresan, dialects of which are also spoken in neighboring Laguna Pueblo as well as in Zia and the pueblos of Santa Ana, San Felipe, Santo Domingo, and Cochiti nearly 100 miles to the east along the Rio Grande. There is some evidence that the Keresan language derived from that of people who inhabited the Anasazi settlement of Mesa Verde in the Four Corners area, and Acoma (and Laguna) historians tell that some of their people came from there. Today virtually everyone at Acoma also speaks English, and some use of Spanish persists.

When the Spanish arrived, a hundred or so families lived in the high pueblo of Acoma, which was accessible only by steep trails cut into the side of the mesa, up which such essentials as water had to be carried, usually in pots on the heads of women. The village consisted of houses in parallel rows, entered from above by ladders. Weaving, pottery, and basketry were practiced, along with horticulture. On numerous farm plots and smaller farming settlements on the lands below, both dry farming and ditch irrigation were practiced; these produced bountiful crops of corn, beans, melons, and squash. The high pueblo was the political and religious center of all tribal activities.

The Acoma people adopted sheep- and cattle-raising from the Spanish, along with the cultivation of various vegetables and orchard fruits, and took up the use of silver as well. Over the years, the Spanish made sporadic attempts to put Acoma under its yoke and Christianize it; there were instances of nearly unspeakable Spanish brutality, periods of wary acceptance and peace, and times when the Acoma, often violently, threw the Spanish out—one of those times being in 1680, when Pueblo people from Taos to Hopi drove the Spanish from the region.

Throughout this long period of alternating peace and tumult with the Spanish, to which was added occasional raids by neighboring Navajos, the Acoma people developed a deep-seated suspicion of outsiders that persisted long after New Mexico became part of the United States in 1848. Acomas zealously guarded their own ceremonial and religious practices, keeping much of their cultural lives secret. To this day much of Acoma life—particularly its ceremonial life characterized by song, dance, and drama—remains unknown to the outside world. The tribe has maintained some Roman Catholic practices, including marriage rites; the pueblo celebrates September 2, the feast day of St. Stephen, as its saint's day.

Today, most of the Acoma people (about 2,600) live in settlements like Acomita and McCarty's down below, but maintain familial houses in the high pueblo, which is used chiefly as a ceremonial center. Government offices (the tribe is run by an elected governor and appointed council) and hospital and other services are also operated in settlements below.

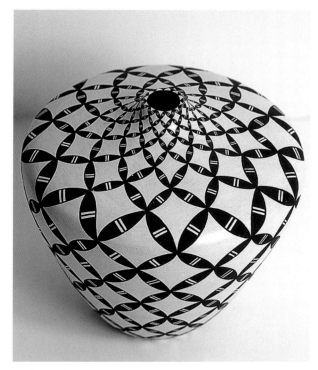

Pot by Dorothy Torivio. Acoma.

dealer Jill Beach, this is not viewed as having less value by many buyers of Acoma pots, who are more interested in the delicate drawing and complex designs than in the materials used.

Plate by Sharon Lewis, Acoma.

mixed with crushed potsherds as temper. Black paint is made from crushed hematite rock mixed with beeweed.

Another popular style is corrugated pottery (based on Anasazi antecedents) made by building up fine, unsmoothed coils that are textured with a pointed tool. Large water jars are often made this way.

Although some Acoma potters today use greenware that is then painted and fired, according to East Coast

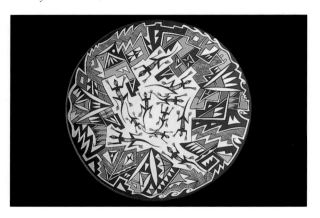

COCHITI POTTERY

A dominant feature of Cochiti ceramics is the storyteller, invented by Helen Cordero in the 1960s and now highly popular here and in several other pueblos (for example, Jemez). Storytellers, reflecting the tradition of elders telling stories to children, usually have their eyes closed, their mouths open; they can also be animal figures. They are typically made with black and red on cream slip.

Cochiti potters often use clouds, lightning, and rain motifs not seen on most other Pueblo pottery. Traditional Cochiti pottery has black designs on a cream slip with some reds added to the design. A red slip may be added to the bottom and to the interior.

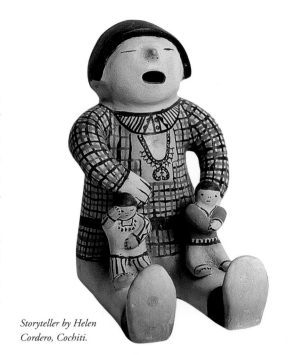

Storyteller by Helen Cordero, Cochiti.

COCHITI PUEBLO (PRONOUNCED COE-chi-tee)

Some twenty-five miles southwest of Santa Fe, Cochiti Pueblo is in the lee of an enormous earthen dam built by the Army Corps of Engineers in modern times to create Lake Cochiti, a chief regulator of the flow of the Rio Grande. One entrance to the village is presided over by a large water tank painted to resemble one of the drums for which Pueblo craftsmen are noted. The pueblo itself is a town of recently built residences widely spread out around an older plaza, itself the center of various priestly and community buildings, along with the Mission of San Buenaventura. The village is central to a reservation of some 50,000 acres that is bisected by the Rio Grande.

One of the Keresan-speaking tribes, the Cochiti people, now numbering under 1,000, trace their history back to a sojourn in an extensive urban-style pueblo carved into the lava cliffs of Bandelier National Monument's Frijoles Canyon. Before the arrival of the Spanish they had taken up residence in their present location and practiced a relatively simple agriculture with simple equipment, as well as hunting game in the nearby Jemez range. Ceremonial practices and social organization were similar to those of the other related tribes—a matrilineal society characterized by clans and also membership in the dual, or moiety, system of religious societies, these latter given over chiefly to healing functions. As with many other of the Pueblo peoples, particularly the eastern ones, the Cochitis have kept their ways largely to themselves. (At one time they apparently went so far as to invent a large number of fallacious details to feed to an interested ethnologist.) As elsewhere, the katsina and medicine society rituals have always been closed to non-believers, while other ceremonies—agricultural rites now blended with the Roman Catholic calendar—have been open. Most notable is San Buenaventura's feast day, July 14: a morning mass followed by a daylong Corn Dance in which the two main kiva groups—Turquoise and Pumpkin—participate. It takes place first near the church, then in the plaza.

Today, tribal members speak mostly English, and many live off the reservation, returning for religious and other observances. Traditional agricultural practices have, in recent times, declined along with many of the early ceremonial practices that were geared to the agricultural year. A greater reliance on the cash economy of the outside world has gone hand in hand with more modern, mechanized forms of agriculture practiced on lands now regularly and predictably watered via the new dam.

Most notable today among Cochiti crafts is the making of storytellers, a Cochiti innovation.

HOPI POTTERY

The clay used by Hopi potters has the unusual ability to achieve various colors upon firing, depending on its iron content and the level of heat. Yellow clay makes red pottery; gray clay produces a range from yellow to peach to light orange, and these hues may be present in the same pot. Many pots are made without a slip, since the clay can be given a fine sheen—almost a golden glow—by stone polishing.

Complex, swirling designs filling the available field are characteristic—black and red and occasionally white, often outlined in a fine black line. Some areas within a design may be stippled black or tan. Some Hopi potters use a white slip and paint designs in red and black.

Frequent design elements include geometrics and highly stylized birds and feathers, butterflies, katsina faces, along with various animals and the Hopi sun. Shallow bowls are usually decorated on the inside, pots on the outside.

This highly recognizable tradition stems from the rediscovery in the late nineteenth century of pottery from a Hopi village, Sikyatki, near First Mesa, that had been abandoned in the early 1600s. A Hopi-Tewa woman, Nampeyo, and her husband, Lesou, studied the old shards and found the old sources of clay. Nampeyo's pottery soon became world famous, and her descendants—notably Dextra Quotskuyva—and other potters have continued in much the same vein, making creative use of the prehistoric design elements. (These same elements are common in other Hopi crafts, particularly Hopi jewelry.)

Unsigned canteen, 1930s, Hopi.

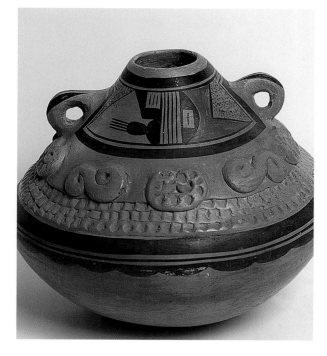

Pottery traditionally has been done by women from the First Mesa villages—Walpi, Sichomovi, and Hano, and Polacca down below the mesa. (Basketry is the preserve of Second and Third Mesas.) In recent times, however, a number of young Hopi men have successfully taken up the art.

Most Hopi pottery is still made in the traditional manner: black paint comes from an extraction of tansy mustard mixed with hematite rock, red from an iron-rich clay. The preferred brush for painting is a finely fashioned strip of yucca. Pottery is fired in sheep manure and locally dug coal.

Read more about Hopi culture in the Carvings chapter (pages 48–49).

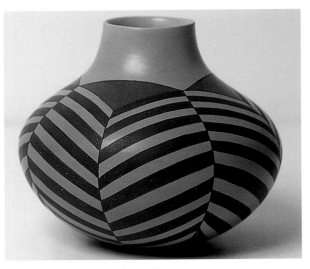

Seed pot by James Garcia Nampeyo, Hopi.

Modern pot by Dextra Quotskuyva, Hopi.

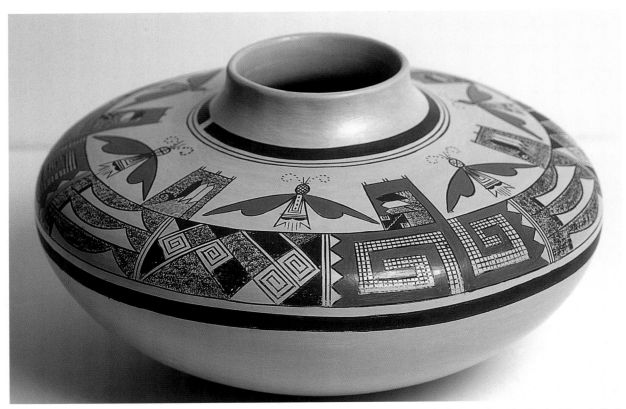

RIGHT: Black-on-white pot by the late Helen Naha (Feather Woman), Hopi.

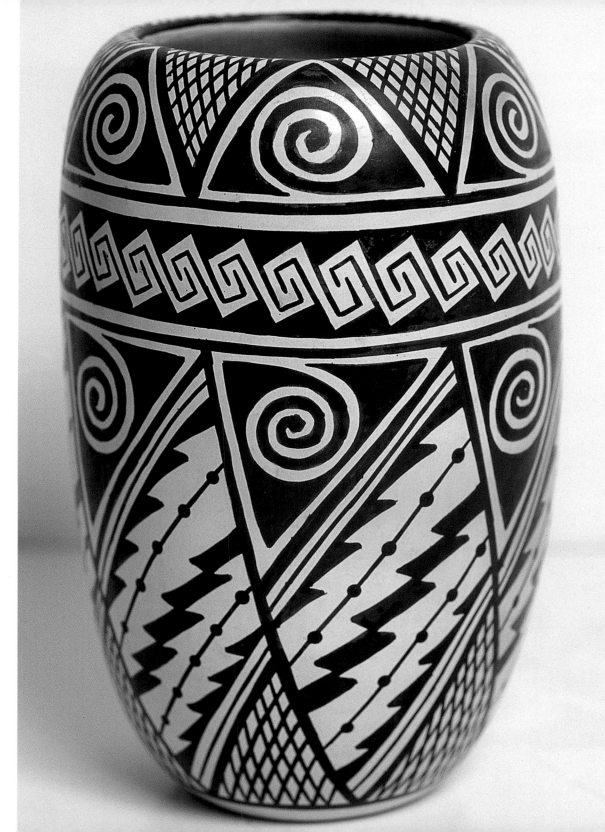

ISLETA POTTERY

The few potters at this polyglot pueblo tend to follow the lead of Acoma and Laguna in pottery design.

Commonly, a white-slipped pot of local reddish-brown clay is given a red base, with the red and black designs mentioned above. Brown, orange, and pastels are also used.

In earlier times Isleta pottery was straightforward redware made from relatively poor-quality brown clay. When Laguna refugees arrived in the 1880s, Laguna styles and techniques were adopted, but pottery-making soon died out and was only recently revived in a limited range.

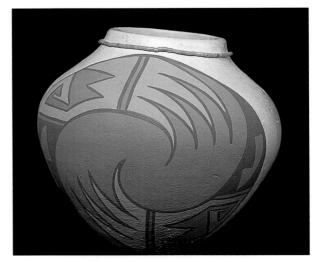

Pot with turquoise "necklace," by Stella Teller, Isleta.

ISLETA PUEBLO (PRONOUNCED IZ-LET-TA)

The long and narrow Isleta reservation (some 211,000 acres) lies like a giant dam across the Rio Grande Valley just south of Albuquerque. The main village, Isleta, is a place of mostly modern structures on the east bank of the river and is called Siehwibag in the tribe's Tiwa dialect, itself part of the Kiowa-Tanoan tongue that is spoken by most of the non-Keresan Pueblos of this region.

In prehistoric times, Isleta grew from a gathering of many related villages in the nearby area, some of these having derived from Anasazi roots, others from Mogollon roots. Isleta did not join in the Pueblo Revolt of 1680; indeed, some of its members soon were taken by the Spanish south to El Paso, and they established a pueblo there. Some people in the neighborhood fled to Hopi (along with some from Sandia) but in about 1740 were sent back and were temporarily joined by some converted Hopis. The present village of Isleta may have been established around this time.

More than a century later, Isleta Indians received into their midst some dissident Laguna people, who brought with them new craft styles.

Like many of the Pueblo peoples, Isletans have guarded the details of their ceremonial life closely, but it appears to consist of several Corn societies—something like katsina societies—that put on unmasked dances associated with rain for Isletan fields, which have long produced traditional crops by ditch irrigation. Historically, in addition to raising some Spanish crops, the people of Isleta grew grapes and traded these (and wine) with other Pueblos. Also, they hunted in the nearby Manzano Mountains and fished in the Rio Grande.

Isleta society honors both the mother's and the father's side, but the emphasis is patrilineal (use of farmland is inherited through the father, for example). Evidently there are no clans, but a child belongs to either the summer or the winter moiety, and through it participates in the tribe's ceremonial life.

Until the middle of the twentieth century, political leadership was split uneasily between religious and secular leaders, but the latter now operate under a democratic constitution. Today, many of the 3,000 Isleta Indians have sought jobs off the reservation in Albuquerque and elsewhere.

JEMEZ POTTERY

Jemez potters use traditional materials and techniques to make pots in a recently developed style characterized by buff and red slips with designs in red, buff, white, and black. Design elements are geometric, often symbolic of moisture—notably clouds and lightning—and often quite "busy."

Several Jemez potters, notably the daughters of the late Mary Toya, make storytellers painted brown, black, and red on a buff slip.

JEMEZ PUEBLO (PRONOUNCED HEY-muss)

The Jemez Pueblo is located at the mouth of a beautiful canyon through which the Jemez River descends. The Jemez people trace their origins to a place, probably Stone Lake, far to the north in what is now the Jicarilla Apache Reservation. There they lived 2,000 years ago, moving south to their present place perhaps in response to the arrival of the Apaches in the area. In any event, by the time the Spanish arrived in the sixteenth century, the Jemez people lived in some ten villages located mostly in the nearby Jemez Mountains. They were, among Pueblo peoples, *the* mountain dwellers, and as such relied less on farming than the others.

Their language is Towa, one of the Kiowa-Tanoan tongues of the northern Pueblos, and some of these Towa-speakers also settled to the north and east, at Pecos, which was abandoned after the Pueblo Revolt of 1680.

Relations with the Spanish were tumultuous, alternating between periods of reluctant acceptance and outright violence. Catholic missions were established, and Catholicism added to the people's traditional religious life. A Spanish form of secular governance was introduced and added to the traditional theocratic rule. At no time, however, did Jemez abandon its traditional ways.

With the Pueblo Revolt came a period of special tumult and disruption. Relations with Keresan-speaking Zia and Santa Ana neighbors worsened, going from occasional raiding to outright hostilities. A group from Jemez (said to be the Coyote clan) left to live in the north among the Navajos, bringing them Pueblo culture, much of which has been permanently absorbed into Navajo life. Others went temporarily to Hopiland. Many of those among the Navajos intermarried there and remained; others returned to Jemez.

Meanwhile, throughout this difficult time, Jemez people moved alternately into the mountains and back to their present area, finally settling in the present pueblo located now within one of two large blocks of reservation land totaling about 89,000 acres in all.

At Jemez one is born into a matrilineal clan (which has certain ceremonial roles), while membership in either the Squash or the Turquoise moiety derives from the father's line. The moieties are responsible for certain ceremonial affairs, including dances that are usually closed to outsiders. The dances of the Christmas season are usually open to the public. There are also various religious societies, but fewer now than a century ago.

Today, English is widely spoken as a second language, and the Jemez people (about 1,700 strong) have taken an active role in county and school board politics, while many work at jobs off the reservation.

Wedding vase by Juanita Fragua, Jemez.

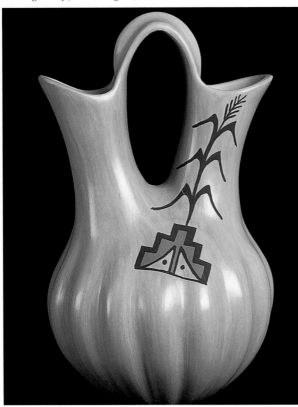

LAGUNA PUEBLO
(PRONOUNCED LAH-GOO-NAH)

About forty-five miles west of Albuquerque on U.S. Route 40, the main pueblo of the Laguna tribe rises on a small hill to the north, the trim, serene village topped by a Spanish mission church. Today the old pueblo is surrounded by a small sea of modern housing, and the reservation includes six other major settlements like Mesita and Paraje.

Always something of a melting pot, Laguna (population about 7,000) is home to one of the most numerous of New Mexico's nineteen Pueblo tribes and has the largest reservation land area (460,000 acres). Of the nineteen pueblos, it is the only one established in historic times, having been created just before 1700 when a few people from Cochiti, Santo Domingo, and others fled to Acoma to avoid the Spanish, lately returned after being ejected from the territory in the Pueblo Revolt of 1680. They joined some disgruntled members of the Acoma tribe, founded Laguna fourteen miles to the northeast of Acoma, and soon made peace with the Spanish.

Presumably these new arrivals mingled with the Keresan-speaking people who had arrived earlier from the Anasazi site of Mesa Verde, as well as a sprinkling of formerly Hopi people. The Keresan tongue of the prior inhabitants and most of the migrants became the pueblo's language—with English as a nearly universal second language by the latter part of the twentieth century. The name Laguna is from the Spanish mission; the pueblo's Keresan name is approximately *Kawaika*, which may hark back to the name of an earlier Hopi settlement that was abandoned when its residents came to the Acoma region.

The earlier residents of Laguna had, like their Acoma neighbors, long practiced dry farming and ditch irrigation, producing corn, beans, melons, and squash. Laguna soon took up horses, goats, sheep, and cattle from the Spanish, and were regularly raided for these and for slaves by the Navajos and occasionally the Utes from Colorado. (By 1935, Laguna was by far the most pastoral of the pueblos, with herds of more than 50,000 sheep.)

Traditional Laguna ceremonial and religious life was complex and various. A variety of religious societies existed, some of which are akin to those of Acoma. Most are shamanistic in nature, devoted to various forms of healing, with some specializing in caring for the hunt or for warfare.

Ceremonial and religious life was played out alongside a Roman Catholic presence that was, in the late nineteenth century, further stirred up by a group of white Protestants. All this, plus pressure from surrounding Hispanic ranchers and internal pressures, led to a period of great social confusion and upheaval and finally to a tribal split called the Laguna Break. In the late 1870s, some of the Laguna people sought refuge first at Sandia Pueblo, then at Isleta, where they taught Isleta women to make the Laguna black, white, and red pottery. But stress occurred at Isleta, and most of the original Laguna migrants returned to Mesita.

Today, Laguna has become widely acculturated to the outside world, though a good deal of the old ceremonial life has been preserved or, in some cases, resurrected. In the 1970s, many Laguna men worked in two uranium mines (now closed) on Laguna land. The tribal government has developed new business enterprises on the reservation, and, in league with the Bureau of Indian Affairs, an elementary and high school system that has sent many of its students off to colleges and universities.

Traditional-style pot by Wendell Kowemy, Laguna.

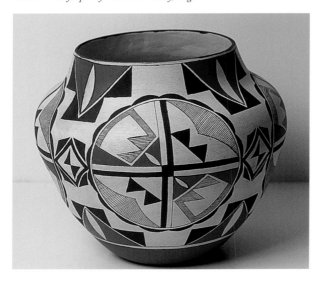

LAGUNA POTTERY

Over the years, Laguna potters have tended to follow the lead of those at Acoma, using much the same techniques, materials, and designs.

Black-on-white, and black and orange (and red and dark brown) on white predominate, with Acoma-like cross-hatching and geometric elements and figures.

Laguna pots tend to be *less* thin-walled than Acoma's. Otherwise distinguishing between the two pueblos' pottery is difficult (one should ask). Black crushed rock is sometimes used instead of crushed potsherds to temper the local clay.

Pottery making died out almost completely at Laguna in the late nineteenth century and well into the twentieth. Its revival began with the work of Evelyn Cheromiah in the early 1970s.

NAVAJO POTTERY

Navajo pottery is traditionally made from coarse micaceous clays that turn to a range of colors from golden brown to an almost charcoal brown when fired. Design is relatively simple—leaves and animals incised or appliqued, or a simple rope-like necklace.

Unique to the Navajos, the pots are sealed with a coating of piñon pitch instead of a glaze to make them waterproof, but it also makes the pots sticky if left in the sun.

A variation on the coiled and smoothed pots is to leave the coils unsmoothed.

Traditional Navajo pot, 1980s, signed "SYC."

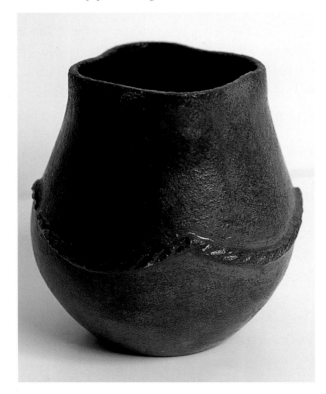

A number of younger Navajo potters have taken up the techniques of the Pueblo potters but using traditional Navajo design elements, such as the highly stylized *yeis,* or Navajo deities, and more representational figures.

Read more about Navajo culture in the Weavings chapter (pages 33–34).

PICURIS PUEBLO
(PRONOUNCED PEE-CYOOR-EES)

Picuris Pueblo lies in the mountainous portion of a 15,000-acre reservation in northern New Mexico, south and east of Taos, with which its people share the Tiwa language, a branch of the Kiowa-Tanoan tongue. A large and thriving pueblo with multistoried buildings at the time of the Spanish arrival, it suffered from raiding and was much reduced in size after the 1680 Pueblo Revolt. Fierce resistance continued after the Spanish return twelve years later, but before long the village was abandoned and its people went to live among the Apaches.

They were repatriated in the early eighteenth century and joined the Spanish in campaigns against the Comanches, Utes, and other raiding tribes. After peace was made in 1780, the Picuris faced another pressure: the encroachment on its land by Hispanic settlers, which continued well into the twentieth century.

Picuris today remains a relatively self-contained community of about 150, enjoying several vestiges of its former cultural life, but also connected to the greater world through jobs in the cash economy outside the community.

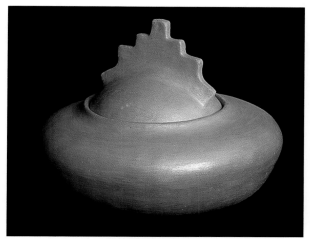

Pot with kiva design, by Ralph Sena, Picuris.

PICURIS POTTERY

Like their neighbors at Taos, Picuris potters use a coarse, local clay flecked with mica to produce a utilitarian pottery that, when fired, ranges through various shades of bronze. Its walls are typically thinner than those of Taos pottery, and the minimalist design is most often a simple appliqued coil or other element.

SAN ILDEFONSO POTTERY

Home to many highly skilled and creative potters, San Ildefonso is best known for the black-on-black ware first created by world-renowned Maria Martinez and her husband, Julian, in 1919. This has a matte black design on a highly polished black pot. It is achieved by painting a clay design on a burnished red pot; in the firing, oxygen is removed by smothering the fire with manure and ashes.

Common design features are the water serpent, called Avanyu, circling the pot, and a stylized repetition of feathers (from prehistoric times). These are found in all the many other styles seen at this pueblo.

Maria's son, Popovi Da, is credited with several other innovations (that is, new traditions). By another firing technique, he created a sienna-on-black ware; he experimented with inlaying pieces of turquoise in pottery; and he also began making pottery in the older San Ildefonso polychrome tradition of black-on-red on a white slip.

Another innovation is carved blackware, begun in the 1930s by Rose Gonzalez and others, which includes

SAN ILDEFONSO PUEBLO
(PRONOUNCED SAN EEL-DEH-FOHN-SO)

Located twenty-two miles northwest of Santa Fe, between Santa Clara and Pojoaque Pueblos, San Ildefonso (its Tewa name is roughly *Powhoge,* meaning where the water runs through) was one of the most resistant to missionary attempts, absorbing Roman Catholic practices into its own ceremonial year only in the twentieth century. At the same time, the pueblo suffered severely from squatters on its land until this was rectified in the 1920s: the pueblo now owns some 26,000 acres. But the squatters' misuse of the land—particularly over-timbering of the surrounding watershed—pressured the pueblo away from traditional agricultural practices and toward participation in the cash economy, especially in the realm of arts and crafts. By the 1930s, San Ildefonso was a well-known center of Indian art (almost half the population was so employed), and this continues to be a major source of employment among the approximately 400 tribal members, along with jobs off the reservation in places such as Los Alamos.

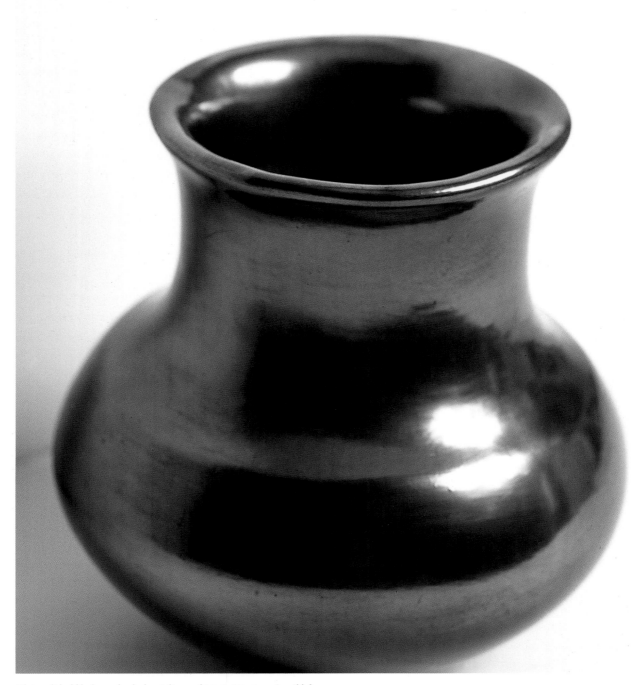

Plain polished blackware by the late Julian and Maria Martinez, San Ildefonso.

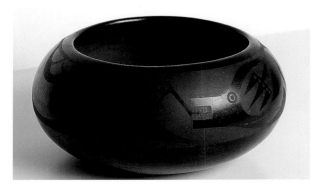

Polished and *matte-finish blackware bowl by Maria Martinez, San Ildefonso.*

figurines and pots carved with various designs. Tony Da specialized in blackware and redware bear figurines with modified heartlines and turquoise inlay.

Yet another favored style is *sgraffito,* in which the surface of a fired pot is chipped or etched to make intricate designs. Many pottery styles and motifs are shared with nearby Santa Clara.

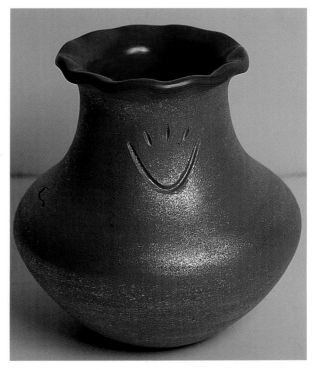

Pot from micaceous clay by Russell Sanchez, San Ildefonso.

SAN JUAN PUEBLO

Northernmost and largest of the Tewa pueblos, San Juan is called *O'ke* (pronounced *o-keh)* in Tewa. Some 1,300 tribal members live on reservation lands of 12,000 acres. The village is located on the fertile, east bank of the Rio Grande just below its confluence with the Rio Chama. This is where the Spanish established their first settlement and provincial capital in 1598 (moving the capital to Santa Fe some twelve years later). San Juan was a focal point of the resistance that led to the Pueblo Revolt, and it was from there that the leader, Pope, sent out the runners who alerted each of the pueblos to the precise time for the uprising.

At several times, notably the 1930s and since the 1970s, San Juan artisans have responded vigorously to the growing market in Indian arts, reviving their own crafts traditions and adding others such as jewelry that were not traditional to the pueblo. Redware pottery, weaving, and painting have become popular. There are many cash fishing tournaments (505-753-6057), and a fee is charged for taking photos or video or for sketching. San Juan is also the headquarters of the Eight Northern Indian Pueblos Council.

SAN JUAN POTTERY

San Juan polished redware characteristically has an unslipped and buff-colored band around the middle on which reddish and light-brown motifs are painted. The incised lines are often highlighted with white, red, and micaceous clay paints.

The designs within the matte-finish band are generally bold geometrics and floral patterns or a series of incised rectangles, chevrons, and cross-hatchings. In spite of such elaborations, San Juan pottery tends to have a serene, conservative look.

The San Juan style was a deliberate revival by several potters in the 1930s, based on shards found in an ancestral pueblo across the Rio Grande dating back to the late fifteenth century. San Juan potters also work in a number of other styles—incised polychrome and carved wares.

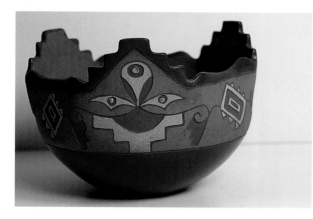

Bowl by Rosita Cata, San Juan.

SANTA ANA POTTERY

Traditional pottery is dominated by grayish-white or buff slip over brick-red clay, with designs executed in red, often, but not always, outlined in dark brown, and black. Bottoms are usually unslipped, showing the red clay.

SANTA ANA PUEBLO

The original pueblo of the Santa Ana tribe, Tamaya, lies in a remote spot in the mesas and foothills of the Jemez Mountains, near where the Jemez River joins the Rio Grande and some twenty-seven miles northwest of Albuquerque. Thanks to its isolation it has been one of the least-visited pueblos and has successfully maintained a cloak of privacy over its affairs. Today, the old pueblo is closed to the public except for feast days and is used almost entirely for ceremonial purposes, and most of the 500 tribal members (while keeping familial homes there) actually live in dispersed homes in Ranchitos, in the vicinity north of Bernalillo along the Rio Grande.

In recent times, Santa Ana has vigorously undertaken a program of economic self-sufficiency through tribal enterprises, including a nursery that retails desert plants for Xeriscape landscaping and the produce from farming carried out on the reservation's 61,000 acres; the emerald-green, eighteen-hole Twin Warriors public golf course along the western banks of the Rio Grande (host to several PGA championship tournaments) at the Hyatt Regency Tamaya Resort and Spa; and the Prairie Star, the resort's European-style restaurant operated under a tribal lease.

In these and other businesses, Santa Ana is among the most enterprising of the pueblos, as well as one of the most private concerning its cultural and religious affairs. Most tribal members are literate in English, and the tribe vigorously encourages its youth to remain in the local schools.

A Keresan-speaking tribe, it reached its present location in prehistoric times, having come from a place members call White House—probably the whitish cliff dwellings of Frijoles Canyon in present-day Bandelier National Monument—where they lived with the people of Santo Domingo, San Felipe, and Cochiti. Before that place, they and other Keresan people probably dwelled in the Anasazi region of Mesa Verde and Chaco Canyon.

As in the other Keresan Pueblos, an individual is a member of a matrilineal clan and one of the two moieties, Pumpkin or Turquoise. There are several associated religious societies, some given over to healing, others to fertility, and much of the traditional religion was linked to the need for rain.

The tribe took part in the Pueblo Revolt; according to one report, all the men left the pueblo to fight the Spanish. Like others, the tribe abandoned the pueblo briefly, but later resettled there and accepted some features of Roman Catholicism into their lives. Today, the feast day of Santa Ana is celebrated on July 26 with a Mass and a Corn Dance not unlike those of the other Keresan Pueblos nearby (Santo Domingo and San Felipe). On June 13, the people go to Sandia Pueblo to the south to celebrate the feast day of San Antonio.

Santa Ana, while producing its own craft items chiefly for private and ceremonial use, also traded for the same things, most notably with neighboring Zia Pueblo. Its craft tradition languished almost to the point of extinction by the mid-twentieth century but has enjoyed a small revival since then.

Design motifs—clouds, lightning, scallops, and triangles—are typically sparse and what has been called "blocky-architectural."

In earlier times, Santa Ana potters followed the lead of Zia, but in the twentieth century the craft was moribund here but for one woman, Eudora Montoya, who began teaching other Santa Ana women in the 1970s. The new pottery harked back to its older design tradition, substituting a fine sand temper for crushed basaltic stone. Clay is obtained near the old pueblo.

SANTA CLARA POTTERY

Santa Clara is a center of highly creative and outstanding potters operating in several traditions. A major specialty is highly polished blackware and redware in graceful shapes.

A Santa Clara innovation, early in the twentieth century, was a bear paw or other design (even simply a coil of clay) impressed into the pot before firing.

Carved pottery was begun by Margaret Tafoya in the 1920s and is widely practiced, along with the technique of *sgraffito,* or etching (after firing), and the creation of matte-finish designs impressed in polished ware, both red and black.

As at San Ildefonso, a favored design element is the water serpent, Avanyu, which is found on both carved and polychrome products. Santa Clara potters have made innovative use of inlaid turquoise and silver, and numerous traditional and nontraditional shapes.

Another major feature is carved figurines, mostly *animalitos* ("little animals"), in polished redware and blackware, often with matte designs etched or impressed into the clay. Figurines are a century-old tradition here.

SANTA CLARA PUEBLO

Known in Tewa as *Xa-po*, Santa Clara Pueblo is located on the west bank of the Rio Grande between Taos and Santa Fe. It is the third-largest of the pueblos, with a population of more than 10,600 and a land grant of some 46,000 acres, mostly rangeland. Within these lands are the spectacular Puye Cliff Dwellings, a major tourist attraction, along with extensive pumice deposits and timberlands that the pueblo leases out.

Having experienced nearly a half century of internal schisms, Santa Clara was the first pueblo to incorporate under the Indian Reorganization Act of 1934. Reorganization provided it with a successful system for maintaining sacred affairs separate from secular considerations. As a result of this, and the rich resource base with which it is blessed, the pueblo is one of the wealthiest and most successful at limiting out-migration. Its crafts are especially highly prized, particularly the famous blackware pottery.

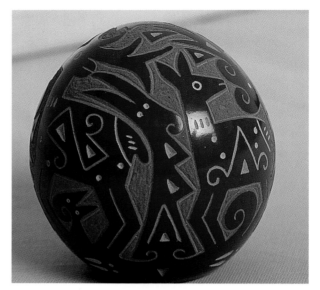

ABOVE: Incised egg by Emily Tafoya, Santa Clara.

RIGHT: Pot by Autumn Borts, of the Tafoya lineage of potters, Santa Clara.

BELOW: Redware wedding vase with sgraffito design, by Celestina Naranjo, Santa Clara.

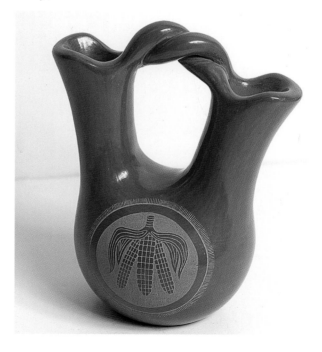

Blackware pot by Belen Tapia, Santa Clara.

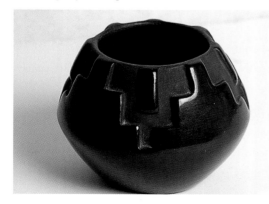

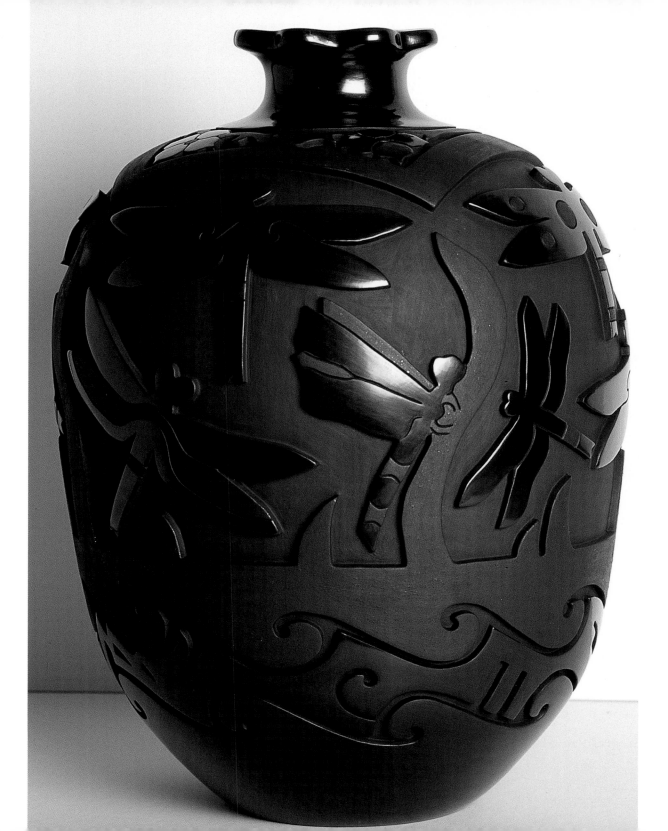

SANTO DOMINGO PUEBLO

A visitor to this pueblo located east of the Rio Grande about halfway between Albuquerque and Santa Fe gets an immediate sense that here is a place of order, prosperity, and tribal self-confidence. The pueblo itself is laid out neatly on north-south and east-west streets with an enormous plaza. To the east is a typical mission church and its *camposanto* (cemetery). Some 69,000 acres of reservation land surround the village and its population of approximately 3,000.

In prehistoric times, the people of Santo Domingo, along with Cochiti, San Felipe, and other Keresan-speaking groups, sojourned in what are the present-day ruins of Frijoles Canyon in Bandelier National Monument before taking up life in their present locations. Keresan is widely spoken still at Santo Domingo along with Spanish and almost universally English as second languages.

A strongly conservative bent has, over the centuries, permitted Santo Domingo to maintain its cultural ways to a degree that is admired by many other Pueblo peoples. Ethnologists and others have been unable to ferret out many specifics about this pueblo's ceremonial and social customs. It is known to be a highly theocratic and structured society.

Paradoxically, a good deal of the people's ceremonial life has accommodated itself to the Roman Catholic calendar, and much of this is, in turn, among the most publicly accessible Pueblo ceremonies. Christmas, New Year's Day, and Easter are celebrated with midnight Mass in the church, after which the patron saint is taken to a shrine in the plaza. Public dances follow through the day. These consist of hundreds of costumed men and women, boys and girls, all from the two main kiva groups, the Turquoise and Squash societies, alternating as dancers in the plaza to the accompaniment of a large band of singers and drummers—altogether an awesome performance. The public is welcome and is expected to maintain a reverent and prayerful attitude. Similarly, the spectacular Corn Dance is celebrated on August 4 annually.

Traditionally, many men of Santo Domingo have acted as traders, bringing Navajo blankets and rugs to the pueblo, for example, in exchange for items like beaded necklaces in demand by other tribes. The necklaces typically consist of small, tubular beads called *heishi* combined with nuggets of turquoise; both men and women at Santa Domingo are especially skilled at making them. One can perhaps see something of the ancient Phoenicians in this entrepreneurial role, the modern ability at Santo Domingo to deal firmly and confidently with the outside world while preserving much of their life as a private affair. At any rate, today Santo Domingo remains highly conservative and protective of its cultural life while engaging, tribally, in various enterprises.

More artwork by Santo Domingo artists is discussed in the chapter on jewelry.

SANTO DOMINGO POTTERY

Large and formal geometric designs executed in bold strokes are a hallmark of Santo Domingo pots. A cream slip on the body and a red slip on the base are common features, as is a red interior.

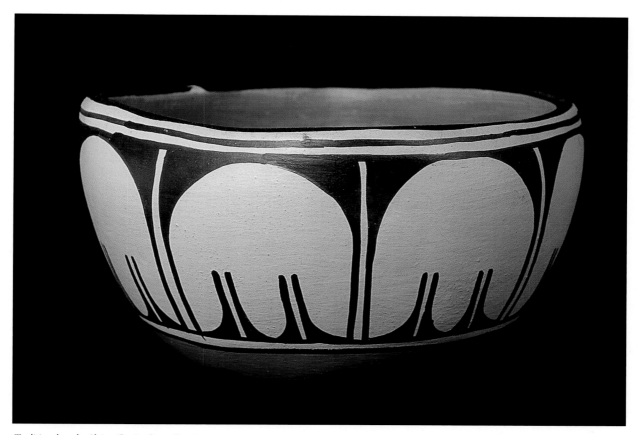

Traditional pot by Alvina Garcia, Santo Domingo.

In addition to geometric designs, the potters favor large floral patterns, birds, and other animals often enclosed within circular bands (with a line break that leaves the circle incomplete). Black lines in a vegetal paint are combined with red.

Santo Domingo pottery is known to be sturdy and durable. The use of red is a modern addition to the nineteenth-century style characterized by black on a cream slip, with bold geometric patterns often repeated all the way around, or two or more such designs in independent units—a style quite unlike that of any other pueblo at the time.

TAOS POTTERY

Taos pottery is straightforward and utilitarian, unslipped, and made from a tan or golden clay filled with flecks of mica (micaceous clay). The mica serves as temper. The pottery fires waterproof and may be oiled inside afterward. The micaceous clay is relatively coarse and not easy to work with; decoration before firing—both incised and appliqued—is minimal.

Taos pottery has been made in this manner since the seventeenth century, perhaps borrowing from the Jicarilla Apaches and Navajos who ranged beyond this northern Pueblo outpost. (Also see Picuris.) Previously, black-on-white pottery was made at Taos.

TAOS PUEBLO (PRONOUNCED TAH-OSE)

With its five-story adobe buildings, Taos is justly famous as the quintessential pueblo, bespeaking an architectural grandeur otherwise found only in ancient places like Mesa Verde. The careful preservation of the old buildings stems from the pueblo's staunch conservatism, which also has kept most of its cultural and religious life from prying eyes and scholarly annals. At the same time, the old pueblo is among those most open to tourism, an apparent paradox but the result of a finely honed ability to keep the sacred and the secular separate.

Taos is a Tiwa language, part of the Kiowa-Tanoan tongue spoken also at neighboring Picuris and, in the south, at Sandia and Isleta. This northernmost pueblo (population today about 4,480) was settled by people who came from the north, presumably Anasazi, and thanks to its elevation (above 7,000 feet) and short growing season, always emphasized hunting over

Storyteller by Karen Tenario, Taos.

Kiva-design pot by Angie Yazzie, Taos.

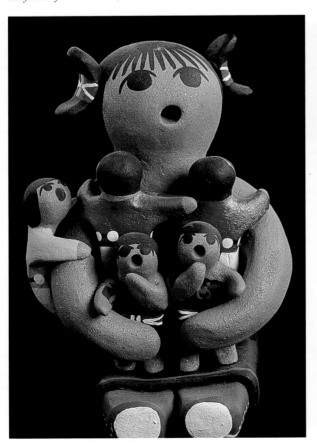

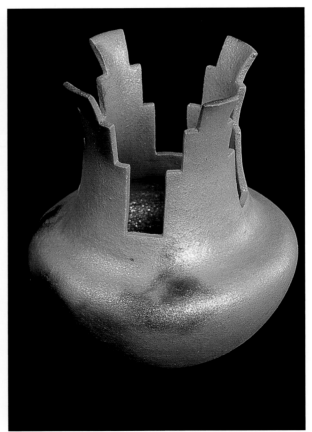

agriculture. The pueblo had considerable contact with Plains tribes, and Taos men seasonally headed east to hunt bison on their own. To this day, most Taos crafts reflect this Plains connection.

Taos was long a hotbed of revolutionary sentiment (it was from a Taos kiva that San Juan Pueblo medicine man Pope led the Pueblo Revolt), and except for an acceptance of Roman Catholicism, the pueblo has resisted influence from either the Spanish or the subsequent American culture. Electricity has been permitted at Taos Pueblo only in the last few decades, and then only in the more modern buildings lying outside the wall that encloses the old pueblo proper. The wall was built originally as a protection against Comanche raids, and today everything inside the wall remains sacred.

All but one of the pueblo's kivas lie within the wall, each kiva's membership having ceremonial functions that are unknown to the others. This compartmentalization of ceremonial function has preserved religious life and a high degree of communalism and mutual reliance, much as the specialized tasks of the Hopi clans do far to the west.

Of the American Indian tribes in the twentieth century who have sought some remedy for the loss of aboriginal lands, Taos is one of the few that received, instead of money settlements, land—in this case Blue Lake in the Taos Mountains and the lands around it. (The reservation now includes about 95,000 acres.) Blue Lake is sacred to Taos and is a seat of ceremonial life, including important tribal initiations.

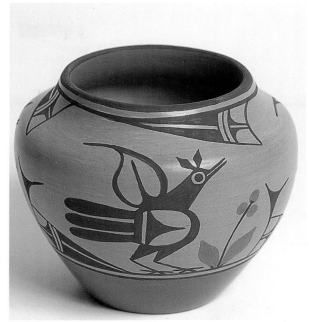

Pot by Eleanor Pina Griego, Zia.

ZIA POTTERY

Major design motifs are a wide, undulating band, often double (and thought to represent a rainbow), that winds up and down from the rim to low on the body of the pot, and a characteristic bird with straight bill, wide eye, and usually forked tail, with grasping claws. Another favored design is a daisy-like flower with large petals, along with other plants, deer, and water symbols.

Designs are usually crisp black and red on a buff or white slip, with the bottom unslipped to show the reddish clay, which is, uniquely, tempered with black basalt. Red and black-on-red are also made.

Zia pots are often thick-walled and hard-fired, and are known for their durability.

Zia pottery today harks back to that made in earlier times when Zia was a major pottery center, trading ceramics for food and other essentials with nearby pueblos.

ZIA PUEBLO (PRONOUNCED ZEE-AH)

Zia Pueblo today is located on the east bank of the Jemez River about thirty miles north of Albuquerque. When the Spanish arrived in the sixteenth century, Zia may have consisted of five separate pueblos with numerous plazas ringed by two- and three-story dwellings and a population in the thousands. By 1690, ten years after the Pueblo Revolt, only some 200 Zians survived in one village, located where Zia Pueblo is found today. Just what combination of Spanish policies and imported diseases led to the greatest decline in numbers of any of the pueblos is unknown. However, almost miraculously, Zia maintained its complicated ceremonial structure of priesthood societies and has kept the mystical side of its life especially private to this day.

Today, some 700 tribal members inhabit a reservation of more than 117,000 acres, one block of which lies across state Route 44 contiguous with the Santa Ana Reservation, with another block beyond the main Jemez Pueblo lands farther north.

The origins of this Keresan-speaking tribe lie with those of the others (particularly Santo Domingo, Santa Ana, San Felipe, and Cochiti) in the present-day ruins of Frijoles Canyon cliff dwellings in Bandelier National Monument. Since prehistoric times, the Zia people have practiced floodwater agriculture along the Jemez River and its tributaries, growing corn, squash, beans, and melons. To these the Spanish added wheat and orchard crops, along with sheep and cattle. Zia gradually became a predominantly pastoral society but maintained its horticultural practices and the religious rites associated so closely with raising crops.

At Zia one is born into one of six matrilineal clans, but ceremonial life hinges on membership in either the Wren or the Turquoise kiva society and in one of eight secret priestly societies. At Zia, while the social order is strictly adhered to and enforced, families are accorded a great deal of privacy: to look through another family's window is to run the risk of being accused of witchcraft. Some of the priestly societies have curative functions—warding off illnesses and epidemics, or witchcraft—and others are devoted to bringing rain and to other agricultural purposes, and perform many legendarily magical feats in the privacy of the kivas. While some of these religious practices seem to be fading away, two separate governing councils remain, one concerned with religious and ceremonial life, the other with secular affairs. In addition to traditional religious practices, the Roman Catholic Church has a continuing presence, and pueblo-wide celebrations mark Christmas and Easter in ways similar to Santo Domingo's. In the happy confluence of both religious traditions, the clown societies, Koshare and Quirana, manage the annual Saint's Day Dance on August 15. Zians consider themselves the most effective dancers among the Pueblo peoples, an opinion shared by many others.

There is also a wholly nontraditional style, practiced by a few Zia potters, featuring multicolored eagles and Pueblo dancers painted in acrylic.

ZUNI POTTERY

Zuni pottery is typically white-slipped with a red base and covered in an elaborate array of black and red designs. A favored element is a deer with a heartline, since the deer showed the earliest-arriving Zunis where to find water in their arid region.

Other design elements include sweeping spirals (called *rainbirds*), various creatures associated with water—dragonflies and frogs—along with stylized feathers and hatching (rain).

Often one or more black lines with a line break encircle the pot near its mouth, with areas set off with vertical lines to display the other design elements.

Pottery of this kind has been revived only recently at Zuni; except for pots made for religious purposes, the craft nearly died out in the twentieth century when jewelry making became the preeminent Zuni craft. The current revival is based on thorough studies of nineteenth-century pottery from museum collections, and that tradition was itself based on Zunis' antiquarian interest in their own prehistoric pottery as seen on potsherds, which were also used as temper.

Modern pot by Anderson and Avelia Peynetsa, Zuni.

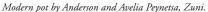

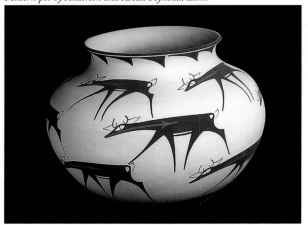

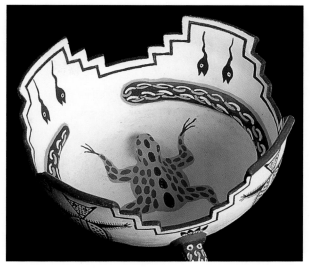

Kiva bowl by Jack Kalestewa, Zuni.

Caveat: The revival of Zuni pottery in the 1970s occurred among high school students, encouraged by two teachers (from Acoma and Hopi) who had a commercial-type kiln installed so the students would not be discouraged in this tricky part of the process. As a result, almost all Zuni pottery today is kiln-fired.

For many years, Zuni potters have made charming, bulbous owls with stubby wings and ears, often with little owls on their backs.

In an altogether separate tradition are small, round pots, often encrusted on the outside with a coating of turquoise grains. These are traditionally vessels for keeping Zuni fetishes.

Read more about Zuni culture in the Carvings chapter (pages 42–43).

CHAPTER FIVE

BASKETRY

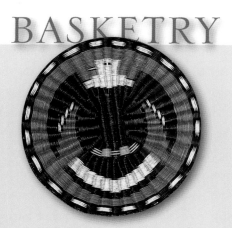

Wicker plaque with eagle design, Hopi.

EXCEPT FOR STONE TOOLS AND HIDES, basketry is probably the oldest human utensil. With something like a basket, one would immediately be a more efficient gatherer of nuts, berries, and fruits. We will never know, probably, since baskets, being made of vegetal materials that rot, tend to decompose over time, and rarely fossilize. In any event, for most of the unimaginably long time *Homo sapiens* has existed (some 100,000 years), the major part of our nutritional sustenance has probably been brought home in baskets.

Given the typically dry climate of the American Southwest over the millennia, the archaeological record of basket making stretches back some 8,000 years. Indeed, several chronological categories of cultures in the ancient Southwest are known to archaeologists precisely from the styles employed in making baskets.

Baskets were made from a host of local grasses, sturdy leaves of desert plants, and the woody shoots of shrubs. They were often decorated with dyes derived from yet other plants. They performed numerous tasks from the practical to the ceremonial and came in many shapes, from conical hats and large burden baskets to water jars (covered with pitch or fruit mush that would harden and seal every opening) and platelike plaques for everything from sifting grain to satisfying the requirements of religious rites.

With the manufacture of pottery in the Southwest in about A.D. 100, some of the functions performed by baskets could be handled more easily by ceramic containers. Properly fired, a clay pot will hold water without leaking or rotting. But baskets—comparatively light and less breakable—continued to find wide use. In our era of plastic plates and shopping bags, the basket has lost much of its utilitarian importance. With exceptions, most of those made in the Southwest are made for sale. They are objects of a simple beauty painstakingly arrived at but also reminders of an earlier time when the hours spent making a practical utensil resulted as well in the creation of art.

To get ready to make a basket, the basket maker may have to travel great distances at different times of year to collect the natural materials—willow, yucca, various grasses—in the proper season. Today even the most accomplished basket makers, whose work appears in museum collections, can barely earn the minimum wage from their art.

MAKING BASKETS

When a Hopi woman from Second Mesa needs to pay back the gifts received by her daughter (at a dance or her wedding), tradition insists that she produce a coiled, plate-like plaque. These are typically made from the leaves and shoots of yucca, a heavily armored desert plant with sharply pointed leaves. So she must spend hours in the desert flats, reaching into these sharp-pointed leaf clusters and getting stabbed and scratched to bring home her

materials. They must be laid out in serried rows to dry, taking up as much space as a modest bedroom. Some will then be dyed with plants gathered from the surrounding area and boiled.

Only then does the making of the actual plaque begin. Depending on size, this may take weeks, the work accomplished while watching TV or in silence, or in sociable groups similar to quilting bees. If such a "payback" plaque is not forthcoming within a reasonable amount of time, the woman's dedication to the proper Hopi Way will be the subject of questioning, one of the most common Hopi national pastimes.

Some Southwestern Indian women (few men make baskets) find the time and the need to make baskets for commercial trade, since each one takes just as long to make as one devoted to a traditional social, ceremonial, or utilitarian purpose.

TWINING

The earliest baskets in the Southwest were twined—a technique of interweaving akin to tapestry. For most of the centuries between 6000 and 2000 B.C., this was the

Plain twining.

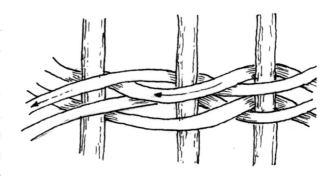

common method, employing shoots of willow, sumac, and other bushes for warps, and split shoots to make flexible pieces for wefts. Innumerable variations on this theme were used. But a new style, perhaps brought from the north, was far more in use by 2000 B.C.—coiled baskets.

COILING

In this technique, the basket maker takes a bundle of twigs, or twigs wrapped in grasses. Beginning with a spiral, she wraps the bundle with a long strand of grass or yucca. Each extension of the bundle continues the spiral outward, while it is wrapped with strands that are sewn

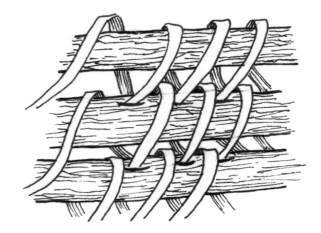

Wicker plaque from Third Mesa, Hopi.

illustration, top: Coiling.

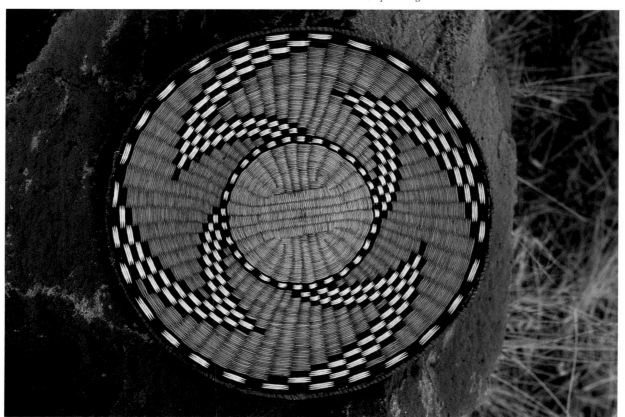

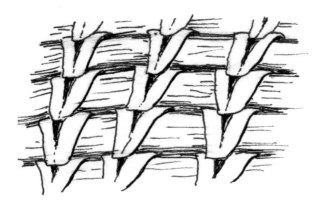

Split-stitch coiling.

onto the center disk with each extending for part of the spiral. This is a simpler task than twining and permits use of shorter and rougher materials.

By about 200 B.C. three types of coiling were practiced, and all have survived to this day. *Three-rod coiling*, in which three rods are wrapped in a triangular bunch, makes a substantial, thick-walled basket of the kind still made by the Western Apaches and the Yuman tribes. *Stacking* the three rods and wrapping them produces thin, flexible baskets and is used by the Mescalero Apaches, the San Juan Paiutes, and the Navajos. The use of *no rods*—only bunches of fibers like yucca or bear grass, which are then wrapped—can make thin or thick coils and is practiced by the O'odham and the Hopi. In this form of coiling, the wrapping stitches can be loose (that is, relatively far apart) and/or split, which is common among the O'odham, or tight, which is found among the Hopi.

Traditionally in the Southwest, the coiled spiral grows from right to left—the direction being figured when facing the work surface, which is usually smoother and more regular than the other side.

BUYING BASKETS

Each tribe has its own criteria for excellence in basket making—the tight stitching of Hopi coiled baskets is not something so avidly sought by O'odham basket makers, who are more likely to experiment with a variety of stitching. The earmarks of any good basket are consistency of stitching and clarity of designs. In some cases (again, such as O'odham or Havasupai) the fineness of stitching and the thinness of coils are important criteria.

FAKES

As noted in the Introduction, imitation "Apache" and "Paiute" baskets are being made in Pakistan and often appear in mail-order catalogs accompanied by such vague phrases as "lovingly handcrafted by families that have been making baskets for centuries." An unwary reader may not notice that the copy does not specifically say that the baskets are made by the Southwestern Indian tribes, and it usually does not specify what they are made of, which is also a tip-off.

These knockoffs take away sales from the Indian people, of course, and also tend to depress prices even for authentic pieces. On the Tohono O'odham Reservation, for example, even young *boys* are beginning to learn to make baskets that can bring in between $1 and $3 an hour—better than nothing at all. Very few Indian artisans of any tribe can support themselves by their art alone, but for most it is a highly significant part of their livelihood. Avoiding fakes and buying authentic pieces is very important to ensure the well-being of these people.

An unusually low price can be a giveaway, as in other fakes and imitations. And, of course, any buyer is entitled to full information as to tribe, basket maker, materials. No seller should hedge about such matters (except that the maker of an old basket may be unknown).

WESTERN APACHES

By 1700, the various bands and groupings of Apaches who later came to be referred to as the Western Apaches laid claim to a territory stretching from the Mogollon Rim (the southern edge of the Colorado Plateau) south to the Gila River. Hunters and gatherers, they took up agriculture as well—perhaps having learned it from the Navajos or the western Pueblo people—and grew limited amounts of maize, beans, and squash. With the arrival of the Spanish and introduction of the horse, they also became adept raiders of any and all neighbors, Indian and European. Spanish settlement never penetrated far into their territory, and they were largely free of Mexican and then Anglo interference until gold was discovered in the 1860s in the north. In the 1870s, the U.S. Army set aside two reservations, one at Camp Verde, the other at San Carlos, for the five different groups of Apaches. By the late 1870s, not only Western Apaches but Chiricahuas from farther east were uncomfortably sequestered in close proximity to each other. Cattle raising became the economic mainstay in both the White Mountain and San Carlos reservations, along with timber in the mountainous north. Missionary efforts have led to fairly widespread acceptance of Christian beliefs, but neither these nor Western medical practices have supplanted the continuing use of shamans for healing certain ailments.

The Pueblo people of New Mexico produce relatively little basketry. Outside of the Jicarilla Apaches in northern New Mexico, this art flourishes chiefly among Arizona tribes.

WESTERN APACHE BASKETS

Once the makers of a vast array of coiled and twined baskets for a multiplicity of purposes, the Western Apaches now produce mostly a few kinds of twined baskets for their own use. Burden baskets still find use in Apaches' ceremonial life; modern ones are more conical than earlier ones and are made for the trade as well. The metal cones on the fringes, perhaps borrowed in earlier times from the neighboring Chiricahua, were intended to rattle loud enough to keep bears away.

Also seen are vase- and bottle-shaped water jars made from sumac and covered inside and out with melted pitch.

Burden basket, signed "Enfield," Western Apache.

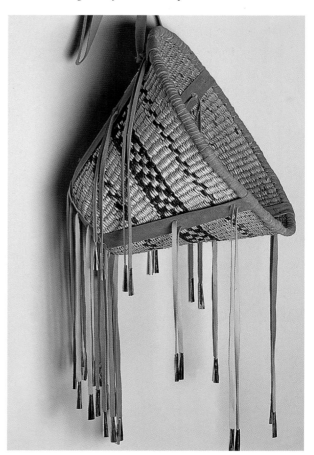

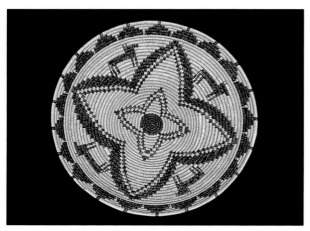

Western Apache basket with common four-petal design and deer, 1920s, artist unknown.

In San Carlos, shallow coiled baskets (often twelve inches in diameter and two inches deep) have been revived; they are usually made with white cottonwood stitching over willow or cottonwood rods. The stitching is even and evenly spaced. A variety of designs, often geometric and petal-like, ranging from simple to complex, are common, as are representations of animals like the wolf.

JICARILLA APACHE BASKETS

The coiled baskets of the Jicarilla Apaches are typically large and strong, with bold geometric designs, often almost gaudy in color. They are usually thick-coiled, with

JICARILLA APACHES (PRONOUNCED KEE-KA-REE-YA)

Given the name Jicarilla from the Spanish name for a small hill in their territory, the Jicarillas speak of themselves as *Haidayin,* "people who came from below."

The Jicarillas may have arrived a bit later in the Southwest than the other Southwestern Apaches, settling in an area that combined both high-plains country (eastward into Kansas) and the southern end of the Rocky Mountains. Some Jicarillas took up a more or less sedentary lifestyle, influenced by the northern Pueblo people; others adopted a Plains-type semi-nomadism, pursuing the great herds of bison. The two groups came to be called Potters and Plainsmen.

The Potters, however, hunted in the mountains as well as practicing irrigated agriculture, living in flat-roofed houses along rivers. Meanwhile, the Plainsmen adopted the tepee and raided, and were raided by, the neighboring Plains people, usually for horses.

In the eighteenth and nineteenth centuries, the Jicarillas were gradually squeezed by Comanches and Utes, and by white settlers, with the Jicarillas alternately aiding and raiding their oppressors. In 1883, all the Jicarillas were moved to the Mescalero reservation, but in 1886 a reservation was established for them in northern New Mexico, straddling the Continental Divide—a rugged terrain of upland canyons and forest. In the short growing season, farming was not productive, so raising cattle became the basis of the economy. This was supplemented in the latter half of the twentieth century by the leasing of gas and oil rights.

The town of Dulce became the main population center and the tribal capital for the approximately 2,000 Jicarillas. Today, the Jicarillas have shifted their economy from livestock to hunting and camping and other recreational activities. The old ties to the extended family have been weakened, with the tribal government taking on numerous responsibilities for the welfare of children and older tribal members.

three and sometimes five sumac rods. The sumac stitching is clear white that turns amber with age.

In the first half of the twentieth century, this craft almost perished, but it was revived upon the creation of a tribal museum and the Jicarilla Arts and Crafts Shop (505-759-4274). Today, commercial dyes are used by most basket makers. Shallow bowls from about fourteen to seventeen inches in diameter are most frequently seen, but Jicarilla baskets are often hard to find off the reservation.

HUALAPAI BASKETS

Hualapai baskets were once both twined and coiled, the more utilitarian baskets being twined. Twined basketry was largely dropped early in the twentieth century in favor of more salable coiled baskets. Since the 1960s, the few Hualapai basket makers have returned to twining for the most part, producing characteristic twined bowls along with water bottles, circular trays, and burden baskets. Designs, usually simple rows of diagonal slashes or zigzags but also using stars and animal figures, are made by alternating diagonal and plain twining.

THE HUALAPAI PEOPLE (PRONOUNCED WOLL-A-PIE)

The name of this Yuman tribe, possibly derived from the neighboring Mohave people, means "pine people," and the Hualapai dwelled for about a thousand years over a large territory west of the Havasupai, much of it in pine-covered highlands. They lived in mobile camps of some twenty-five people, each with its own headman, and the camps united as needed into bands. These were loosely associated in three sub-tribes—the Yavapai Fighters in the south, the Middle Mountain people, and the Plateau people—but formed a single cultural unit whose members called themselves "people"—meaning, essentially, chosen people.

Each camp ranged widely within a given territory, hunting and gathering, and, particularly along rivers, they grew corn, beans, and melons, using dams and springs to create an irrigation system. Religious life was characterized chiefly by shamanism, employed mostly in healing rites. Little else of Hualapai cultural life survived the forced contact with Europeans.

The Hualapai people's first such contact—in 1776—was a Spaniard, whom they killed. They remained free of further contact until the U.S. Army began exploring the region in the 1850s before the railroad came. Such expeditions were met with continuing and escalating hostilities until the Hualapais were conquered and, in 1871, interned for three years in a reservation along the Colorado River. They escaped and returned to their ancestral lands, by then largely taken over by cattle ranches. In 1883, a 900,000-acre reservation was established for them there, but it had been overgrazed and could not support traditional Hualapai life. Most Hualapai declined to live there, seeking work in nearby towns and cities. Many returned during the Depression, and in the 1970s the tribal government—helped with an award from the U.S. Indian Claims Commission—began to create various tribal enterprises, including a doll factory, a trading post, and a livestock industry. Today, some 800 Hualapais live on a reservation of about 990,000 acres.

THE HAVASUPAI PEOPLE (PRONOUNCED HA-VA-SOO-PIE)

Their name means "people of the blue-green water" and refers to the magnificent waterfalls of Cataract Creek Canyon, where the Havasupai summer home is located—a side canyon to Grand Canyon. Here the Havasupai (a Yuman tribe) practiced irrigation agriculture. Prehistorically (as early as A.D. 600) and up until late contact with Europeans, they ranged over an area of nearly 100 square miles from Grand Canyon's south rim nearly to Flagstaff. These were winter grounds, where they hunted deer, pronghorn, and smaller game.

Throughout these centuries, they were closely allied with the neighboring (and related) Hualapai and often in open hostilities with the Yavapai to the south, but otherwise they lived without much outside contact. An exception was trade with the Hopi, through whom they took on such Spanish introductions as the horse, orchard crops, and cloth.

In the late nineteenth century, white cattle ranchers and miners began squeezing the Havasupai from their wintering grounds. A reservation was established in 1880, comprising merely the canyon itself, and it was not until 1975 that the Havasupai regained some of their lands to the north—in all almost 190,000 acres, with 95,000 acres of Grand Canyon National Park designated for their permanent use.

Traditionally, life was relatively simple, organized around the household—typically a man and his extended family. All family members engaged in agriculture, gathering expeditions, and house building, with men responsible for hunting and making clothes (typically from hides). Women, given chiefly to cooking and childcare, made sleeping mats and a variety of basket types used for such purposes as carrying objects, holding water, drying corn, and boiling.

The major ceremony of the Havasupai was a round dance held at harvest time. Rain dances with masked figures were apparently adapted from the neighboring Hopi but abandoned around 1900, rain being unnecessary for agriculture in the well-watered canyon, where summer rains often created troublesome floods.

In modern times, many Havasupai have found work off the reservation, particularly in Grand Canyon Village, and tourism has become the main source of income. The tribe maintains a small motel in Supai with associated tourist facilities and a campground downriver. The town (population about 450) consists of scattered homes of modern construction located amid small orchards, cornfields, and horse corrals, all linked by a network of irrigation channels and walking paths (there are virtually no internal combustion engines in the canyon). Supplies are brought in by pack trains (the post office is the only one in the United States so supplied).

HAVASUPAI BASKETS

An earmark of Havasupai basketry has always been the comparative fineness of its coiling along with the crispness of design. In its heyday in the 1930s, some basket makers achieved superfine textures with seven coils and nineteen stitches to the inch. Today, some Havasupai basket makers are striving for such fineness again, and increased tourism in their remote canyon village may encourage them to greater achievements.

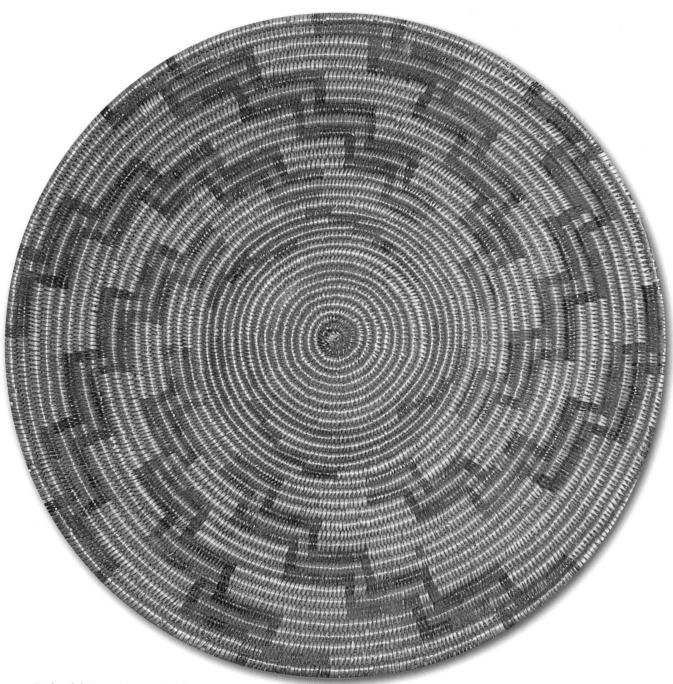

Finely coiled Havasupai tray, artist unknown.

HOPI BASKETS

Plaited baskets, made from yucca over a wicker (now metal) ring and used chiefly as sifters and for parching corn in the sun, are created throughout Hopiland, little changed from those made 1,500 years ago in Arizona. But the women of Second and Third Mesas have traditional specialties in basketry (whereas on First Mesa, pottery is the specialty). In the women's basket dances (usually held in autumn), the women dancers carry all forms of Hopi baskets, which are given away at the ceremony's end.

Coiled baskets and plaques—what scholar Andrew Hunter Whiteford has called "the most elaborate and colorful coiling being done by any North American Indians"—are the specialty of the Second Mesa villagers. They are made of bunches of grass or rabbitbrush, wrapped with strips of yucca that have been dried and dyed as needed. They are notable among the coiled basketry of the Southwest for their often elaborate and colorful designs and thick coils (about a half inch) that are very tightly coiled and stitched.

The outer leaves of yucca are olive green; the inner leaves become white. Others, if bleached, become yellow. Various natural dyes are used to achieve other colors, such as black, orange, and red.

As noted, coiled plaques are used as gifts and in ceremonies, and are also sold.

Plaited wicker baskets are the specialty of women in the villages of Third Mesa. These are made by plaiting

Coiled plaque with the face of a mana, or maiden, Hopi.

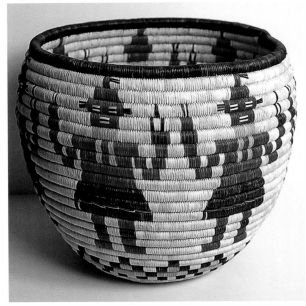

Coiled basket with Mudheads, Hopi. Coiled basketry is the specialty of Second Mesa villages, typically made with bear grass or rabbitbrush wrapped with yucca.

stems of rabbitbrush over and under warps—like spokes radiating from the center—of sumac shoots. Traditionally they are flat plaques or shallow bowls. Like the coiled baskets of Second Mesa, these are widely used in ceremonies and as gifts (or payback for such things as wedding robes).

The variety of designs is vast, and each general design carries a name. Natural dyes are now complemented by aniline dyes to allow the basket weaver a greater variety and brilliance of color than is found in any other Indian baskets.

Read more about Hopi culture in the Carvings chapter (page 48).

NAVAJO BASKETS

Among the many forms of baskets traditionally made by Navajos, including water jars waterproofed with pitch, were shallow coiled trays (usually two-rod coiling) for both healing rites and weddings. Since at least 1890, many of these wedding baskets were made by San Juan Paiutes—with three-rod coiling—and traded to Navajos. These Paiute-made baskets included the break in pattern—a line leading out of the design—that is found in most Navajo rugs as well and for which there are almost unnumbered explanations.

Traditional Navajo baskets had only two colors—black and a deep red—added to the sumac stitching and coils, and rims woven in a herringbone pattern.

By the late twentieth century, particularly in the northwestern part of the reservation near Kayenta and Navajo Mountain, Navajo basketry was seeing a revival in a host of designs, colors, and sizes, and coiled baskets six inches to as much as sixty inches across are made. To traditional designs such as four-petaled starlike patterns, a variety of animal forms have been added, including eagles, butterflies, and *yeis*.

Read more about Navajo culture in the Weaving chapter (page 33).

Navajo wedding basket. The "door" in the design should always face east, like the door of a traditional hogan.

O'ODHAM BASKETS

The Tohono O'odham (Papago) are the most prolific producers of baskets in the Southwest. Their riverine counterparts, the Akimel O'odham (Pima), long shared many of the same basket-making traditions, but the art has largely died out among them and the Tohono O'odham now include formerly Pima designs in their work. The art almost vanished among them as well, but was revived in

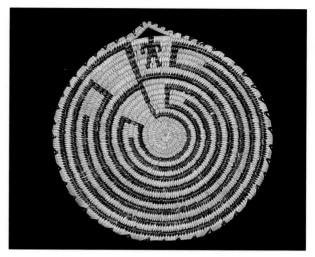

Man-in-the-Maze-design (the main symbol of the Tohono O'odham people), by Frances Manuel, Tohono O'odham.

the 1950s with some help from the American Friends Service Committee. Today, the Hoo-Hoogam Ki Museum on the Salt River Pima-Maricopa Indian Reservation is also encouraging the remaining few Pima weavers by providing them with a reliable market for their work.

Traditional coiled baskets of the Tohono O'odham were made with bunches of bear grass and sometimes yucca sewn with narrow strips (or splints) of willow, the coils then pounded flat with rocks. When visible through the stitching, bear grass is a dark green that fades with age to a yellow tan. Devil's claw was, and is, used for black designs, and the Tohono O'odham use far more black in their designs than their riverine counterparts.

In the earlier part of the twentieth century, when a market demand for their baskets emerged, most Tohono O'odham women switched from willow, which is hard to work with, to the more easily worked and more widely available yucca. They also practiced less-tight stitching to let the bear grass coils show through and soon began splitting the stitches to create a variety of effects. New designs

THE O'ODHAM

By the time the Spanish arrived in the Sonoran Desert of present-day Arizona, the O'odham life was determined largely by the varying degrees of aridity of their very arid territory. In the driest parts—west from about Ajo to Yuma—lived the "no-villagers," or Sand Papago, who led a nomadic existence in constant search of water and food resources (as well as fishing in the Gulf of California for shellfish and other marine life). They evidently traded shells for Yuman pottery and food and lived in small, roving bands, sleeping in circles of stones or brush. This way of life died out altogether by the beginning of the twentieth century.

East of the wholly desolate lands where the Sand Papago eked out a living, the bulk of the Papagos (Tohono O'odham) lived: "two-villagers" who maintained winter homes near permanent springs in the mountain foothills and summered on the plains, where they farmed by channeling summer rainfall into arroyos and down onto the plains.

Villages were made up of a few family households, each family having several buildings for sleeping, cooking, and so on, and each village having public or sacred lands nearby for ceremonial and other purposes. Groups consisting of several villages were named for a local feature, such as a stand of willow trees, and maintained this name regardless of where they might eventually move. Such groups also retained sacred plaited baskets with ancient relics bespeaking the group identity, and these were brought out for ceremonial occasions: rituals associated with the corn harvest, deer hunting, purification events, and the summer feast centered on wine made from cactus fruit.

As is common in high-risk living situations, cooperation and gift giving among households, along with exchange of valuables through wagering, were of paramount importance. For example, a household grew and owned its own food, but custom dictated that once the food was prepared into a meal, it was always doled out to others in the village. Not surprisingly in a highly mobile society not given to elaborate technology, basketry (made by women) was a primary craft.

With the coming of the Spanish in the early eighteenth century, Roman Catholicism was added to Tohono O'odham ceremonialism and shamanism, and the tribe took on Spanish cattle, horses, and wheat crops. The period was characterized by rebellion against the Spanish yoke, and times of "peace," during some of which the Tohono O'odham were enlisted to fight with the Spanish against the Apaches who encroached from the east.

With the coming of the American period in 1848, and once the Apache problem was settled, Tohono O'odham lands were infiltrated by miners, and the Tohono O'odham entered the cash economy, supplying labor to mines, cotton growers, and cattle operations in the region. United States policy created a reservation (a 71,000-acre area at San Xavier) in 1874 and sent Tohono O'odham children off to school—most often Catholic schools elsewhere in the region. By 1916, the government had built more schools (many of them in such distant places as Phoenix) and created two other reservations for the Tohono O'odham, approximately 10,000 acres at Gila Bend and the Tohono O'odham Reservation of 2,770,000 acres around Sells, Arizona.

The major economic activity on this huge area became raising livestock, both individually and as a tribal enterprise, with additional tribal revenues coming from the lease of tribal lands to miners as well as to the National Science Foundation for the Kitt Peak National Observatory. Meanwhile, many of the Tohono O'odham (the tribe has some 17,000 members) now live in Tucson and elsewhere, pursuing work in the cities and returning home for ceremonial and other occasions.

Meanwhile, groups of Akimel O'odham (the Pimas, or "river people") lived along the Gila and Salt Rivers in largely permanent villages. They were the "one-villagers" who lived in a loosely organized society, practicing a stable and comfortable agricultural life made possible by the reliable flow of river water for irrigation. With the arrival of the Spanish, the Pimas began growing wheat (planted in the fall and harvested in spring), which complemented rather than replaced maize, making their fields all the more productive.

With this increased activity, men took on most of the agricultural duties while women produced other items, such as basketry, for commerce that grew as Spanish settlement increased in Tucson and elsewhere.

Meanwhile, the Pima surpluses attracted the attention of Apache raiders, and Pima men often fought alongside the Spanish against the Apaches, a pattern that continued when America won territorial Arizona. Pimas were known as the only effective force for fighting Apaches, and they also became major suppliers of foodstuffs to the U.S. Army and later to miners who began pouring into the area.

But Pima fortunes took a radical downturn when, after the Civil War, white settlers appropriated the waters of the Gila River for their own farms by building canals. As a result the Pima suffered what they call the "years of famine," which extended well into the 1950s, working as day laborers and eking out a living with their Maricopa neighbors on the Salt River Indian Reservation.

have been continually added to the traditional repertoire. Perhaps the most noted traditional design and tribal symbol is the Man in the Maze, or the Home of the Elder Brother. Now one sees various geometrics, life figures, action scenes, birds, cacti, and a variety of desert animals. A popular recent design that has been taken up in pottery and jewelry as well is the friendship dance basket, which shows the backs of a group of men and women joining hands in a circle that runs around the basket.

In addition, O'odham men have long made wire baskets from baling wire; these held food that was lowered into wells to keep it cool and moist. A number of O'odham men continue to make these—from copper wire—for sale. In recent times, some O'odham basket makers have

Friendship dance basket, Tohono O'odham.

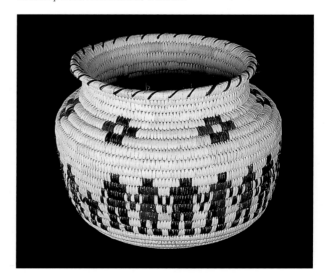

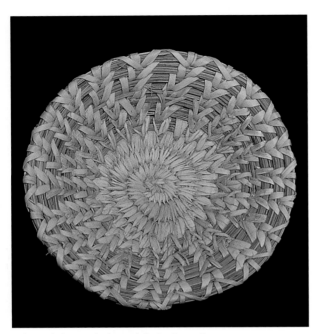

Split-stitched woven basket made by Stephanie Garcia at age seven, Tohono O'odham.

been using horsehair for baskets—particularly miniatures. As Mark Bahti, author and gallery owner, points out, harvesting horsehair for a basket is a great deal simpler than seeking out distant willow, or yucca, and devil's claw, especially for O'odham people who live in or near the city.

SAN JUAN PAIUTE BASKETS

Since the 1890s the San Juan Paiutes have made great numbers of coiled baskets for use by the neighboring Navajos as ceremonial wedding trays. These were typically made with three rods. In addition, they once produced baskets, undecorated or only lightly so, in a variety of shapes and sizes for various internal purposes.

In the 1970s, some of the women from Hidden Springs began dealing with a trader, Bill Beaver, of the Sacred Mountain Trading Post north of Flagstaff. With

his encouragement, Paiute basket makers began making reproductions of the old-time work—conical hats, burden baskets, and so forth. They also began exploring new designs and new colors. The points of the circle on wedding trays began to change, sometimes into Navajo *yeis*. Havasupai-type swirls emerged, and original designs, such as the colorful butterfly baskets, became popular.

The tribe has formed the San Juan Southern Paiute Yingup Weavers Association, a cooperative to advance the art that has become a major source of income for the people, as it once was a basic tool of survival.

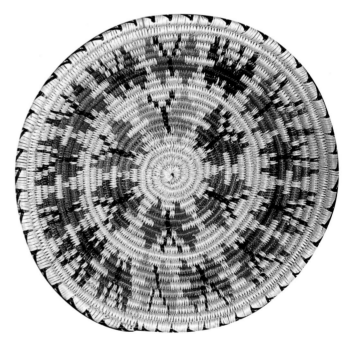

San Juan Paiute butterfly tray.

SAN JUAN PAIUTES (PRONOUNCED SAN WAN PAH-YOOTS)

The San Juan Paiutes are a small group (today, some 200-plus) of a larger group—the Paiutes, who previously lived throughout much of the Great Basin, with their neighboring Shoshones and (to the east) the Utes, all of whom were related by a common language. The San Juan Paiutes are often overlooked in discussions of the Southwestern tribal people, owing perhaps to their Great Basin origins. They are not included in the two volumes on the Southwest in the Smithsonian's *Handbook of North American Indians,* for example, though they live within the northwestern end of the Navajo Reservation. Also, until recently, they have been largely invisible—at least officially. It was only in 1989 that they received official federal designation as a tribe, and for most of the twentieth century they lived in the great shadow cast by the far-more-populous Navajos, well out of the spotlight and influence of the dominant society of the United States.

Since prehistoric times, the Paiutes have practiced a relatively simple culture, eking out a living from their arid lands by some irrigation farming and a great deal of hunting and gathering. While little affected by the few Spanish intrusions into their lands, they were often subject to slave raids by the neighboring Utes and from time to time they preyed on the Hopis.

With the arrival of gold-seekers on their way to California in the 1840s and the subsequent settling of Mormons in their lands, the Paiutes began a downhill slide into dependence and poverty—working at best as farmhands and laborers. Eventually the U.S. government took notice long enough to settle the more northern bands of Paiutes on wholly inadequate reservations in Nevada and Utah, while the San Juan band continued to live just west of the Navajo Reservation on land set aside for them in the Tuba City area. Before long, their territory was added to the Navajo Reservation, and they lived largely unnoticed by the federal government, taking on some of the accoutrements of Navajo culture, from sheepherding to the wearing of velveteen blouses and flowing skirts.

By 1930, the San Juan Paiute population had dropped to some eighty individuals and was still declining. In 1969 the San Juan Paiutes benefited from a larger Paiute settlement awarded by the U.S. Indian Claims Commission, and in 1989 they won federal recognition as a tribe. Today, they are concentrated in two areas on the western Navajo Reservation—northwest of Tuba City and near Navajo Mountain in Utah. There, in the context of extended family ownership, they ranch sheep and cattle, farm, and maintain some of their older ways (including their language), melding them with a Pentecostal Protestantism. Basketry is a major source of income along with their agricultural pursuits.

$\int$

JEWELRY

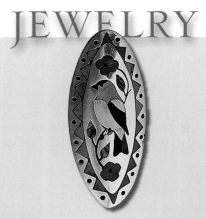

Goldfinch inlaid in silver, purchased in early 1970s, made by Nancy Haloo, Zuni.

AS EARLY AS 300 B.C.—at the beginnings of what became known as the Hohokam culture near the Salt and Gila Rivers in southern Arizona—making objects for personal adornment was already a considerable industry among the indigenous people. Men, women, and children wore a profuse variety of bracelets, pendants, rings, buttons, earrings, and beads fashioned from bone, shell, turquoise, and other materials.

It is clear that such jewelry was highly valued. The shell of choice, for example, was a marine bivalve

(*Glycymeris*), imported by either trek or trade from the Gulf of California. The central portion of one shell half was broken out, leaving the encircling rim, and the edges ground down to make a fine bracelet—all the finer if etched with a geometric design. Some have been found with two pairs of small holes on either side of a break, permitting the break to be stitched together, probably with yucca strips—prehistoric jewelry repair.

Pendants and charms were common—from simple chunks of turquoise or carved bone, or small shells with

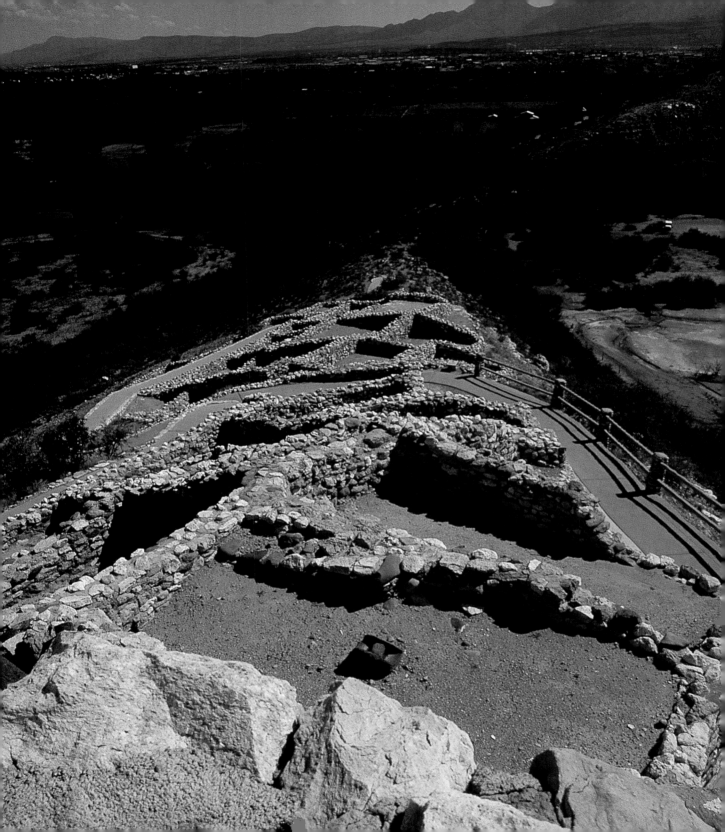

holes drilled in them, to elaborately carved figurines similarly drilled, such as the Hohokam's frog, sometimes found with eyes of inlaid turquoise. Yet another early technique was to overlay a shell or piece of bone with carefully shaped small bits of turquoise and other stone to make a mosaic, held together with pine pitch.

From the Hohokam, jewelry-making techniques and materials spread quickly to the Anasazi people to the north and the Mogollon people to the east. The shells of abalone and spiny oyster *(Spondylus),* both imported from the Pacific, were added as materials and remain favorites two millennia later. Reddish stone called argillite, banded travertine, jet (a lignite product), and many other minerals caught the eye and were made into adornments.

Since those early times, all manner of jewelry has been imported, made, traded, and worn throughout the Southwest—some surely out of pure vanity, some as signs of wealth or status, and some for ceremonial purposes. Copper bells imported from northern Mexico, for example, appear to have been worn only during ceremonial dances. Of all prehistoric jewelry, however, the most common by far were beads—bone, shell, clay, slate, jet, and turquoise, all of which had to be patiently drilled and ground to shape. Drilling such materials was no doubt a time-consuming process, accomplished by three methods: (1) a drill point was attached to a straight shaft and rotated back and forth between the palms of both hands; (2) more efficient was the pump drill, in which a vertical pumping of the crossbar causes the thongs to unwind and wind up, turning the drill; (3) similar to the pump drill is the bow drill, in which the sideways motion of a bow with its bowstring looped around the shaft causes the drill to rotate.

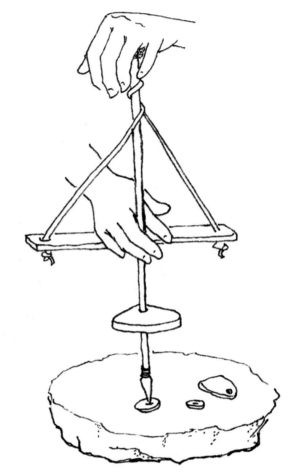

ABOVE: *Pump drill for drilling beads.*

RIGHT: *Zuni-style necklace by Billy Betoney, Navajo.*

Some of these old jewelry styles and jewelry-making methods are still in use. The Spanish introduced silversmithing to the Indians, and over the past century it has been joined by a host of new techniques and materials. But there remains an unbroken chain of events (and human delight) linking the earliest crude pendants of the ancient people of the Salt River to the astonishing array of Southwest Indian jewelry available today.

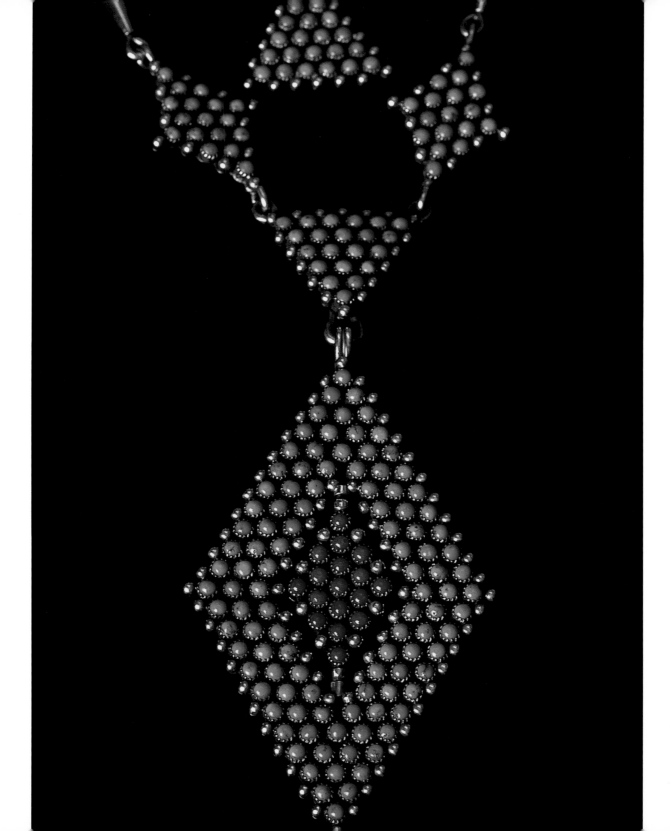

BUYERS' TIPS

Indian jewelry is basically a cottage industry, with the jeweler usually setting up a bench and equipment in a room in the house, such as the kitchen. At its best, it is all handmade, and no two pieces will be exactly alike. In so large and lucrative a trade, however, there are lesser versions or categories, especially copies knocked off from real Indian pieces in factories both here and, increasingly, abroad, in places like Taiwan. They are often found side by side with authentic, totally Indian-crafted pieces. You can sometimes spot the inauthentic pieces because they will all be virtually identical. The "turquoise" or other stones in all the jewelry may be completely uniform. There is nothing illegal in the manufacture and sale of such material, but it *is* illegal to represent it as authentic Indian jewelry.

The Southwestern Association for Indian Arts (SWAIA) and the Indian Arts and Crafts Association (IACA) encourage the trade to be self-policing to ensure that the customer knows what is before him with regard to authenticity. The main category, and obviously most desirable, is what is labeled *Indian handmade.* This means that virtually no part of the piece is made by any means other than the hands of the jeweler. While a few jewelers even hand-roll silver sheets from ingots, most buy sheet silver and strips of silver for making bezels from various jewelry supply houses. Indian handmade jewelry is the glory of the craft.

Another category is *Indian made* or *Indian constructed* or *assembled.* Here the jeweler will purchase machine-made parts—for example, a ring complete with a preformed bezel and a stone to fit the bezel. There is a wide variety of such pieces, called *findings,* and virtually every traditional Indian jewelry form has been reproduced in findings.

The piece may be slightly modified or merely assembled and polished by the jeweler, and several such pieces will look identical. Much of this material is encountered in street sales, in the town plazas, as at Santa Fe, and in most roadside stands and highway fast-food stops.

But as in any human endeavor, there are few generalizations that are without exceptions. The very day we were working out a clever buyer's syllogism ("fast food and fast jewelry"), we encountered, in a large kiosk about thirty feet from the Burger King counter in an enormous Hopi-owned truck stop outside Holbrook, Arizona, a large array of Indian jewelry. Some was made of findings, with some very old and some new handmade pieces including a few by Billy Betoney and the Clarks.

At stores such as Thunderbird Supply and Indian Jewelry Supply in Gallup, New Mexico, findings range from bracelets ready to be inlaid to tiny feathers cast by the lost-wax process in nickel-silver, an alloy of nickel, copper, and zinc—which is to say, it contains *no* silver. Nickel-silver is stronger than sterling silver, but looks like it (just as red brass looks like 14-karat gold). Silver-fill, which is a thin silver plating over nickel, is necessary for engraving because the nickel-silver itself is too hard.

In addition to findings, such supply stores sell virtually every tool a jeweler might need and quantities of pre-cut and polished cabochons of turquoise and other stones, as well as plastic reproductions and thousands of yards of strung "heishi" beads, for the most part cut and drilled in the Philippines. The latter sell for a fraction of what the handmade variety sell for. Also, they sell large quantities of sterling silver in machine-rolled sheets and wire of various dimensions and substances. Virtually no Indian jeweler, says Phil Woodard, of employee-owned Indian Jewelry Supply, rolls his own silver or makes his own wire.

Everything Woodard sells is meticulously labeled as to origin and material. What jewelers do with it then, he says, is out of his control, but he sees nothing wrong with jewelers helping to support their families by assembling

Micro-inlay ring with yei figure, by Carl and Irene Clark, Navajo.

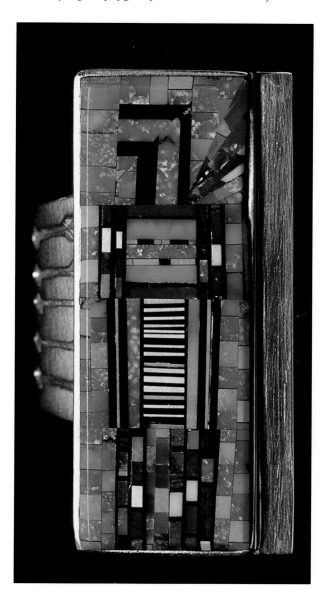

jewelry from such nontraditional components, so long as the product is accurately marked. "Even Filipinos get hungry," Woodard says. In the early 1990s, he helped bring the Federal Trade Commission down on a leading museum shop that was selling in its catalog jewelry made with findings and plastic stones from his store and claiming it was authentic, handmade Indian jewelry.

The entire craft of Indian jewelry, Woodard believes, could not have become what it is today without supply houses and their often less-expensive components. And even the snootiest gallery owner will, if pressed, admit that there is nothing wrong with buying such a product so long as the buyer isn't misled. It is affordable and it does employ people in a region where jobs are not plentiful. (Woodard employs about a hundred people, mostly Navajos.) But it is best to consider it a souvenir; it will not gain value over time as will most authentic, Indian handmade items. And, as with any other kind of purchase from breakfast to a BMW, if in any doubt, ask; you are entitled to the information.

It is harder to inquire from a catalog, of course, and it is important to read catalog copy with extreme care, as the copywriters will often resort to subtle weasel words (or more politely, circumlocutions). A typical example is the following paragraph, quoted from the catalog of a leading national museum's shop, printed next to a photograph of a Southwestern-looking necklace of silver and turquoise.

Our spectacular handcrafted necklace exquisitely showcases the finest veined turquoise of Arizona's famed Kingman mine, which was worked by Native Americans long before the arrival of Europeans. Five large cabochons are hand set into ornamental sterling silver bezels and hand polished to a brilliant sheen.

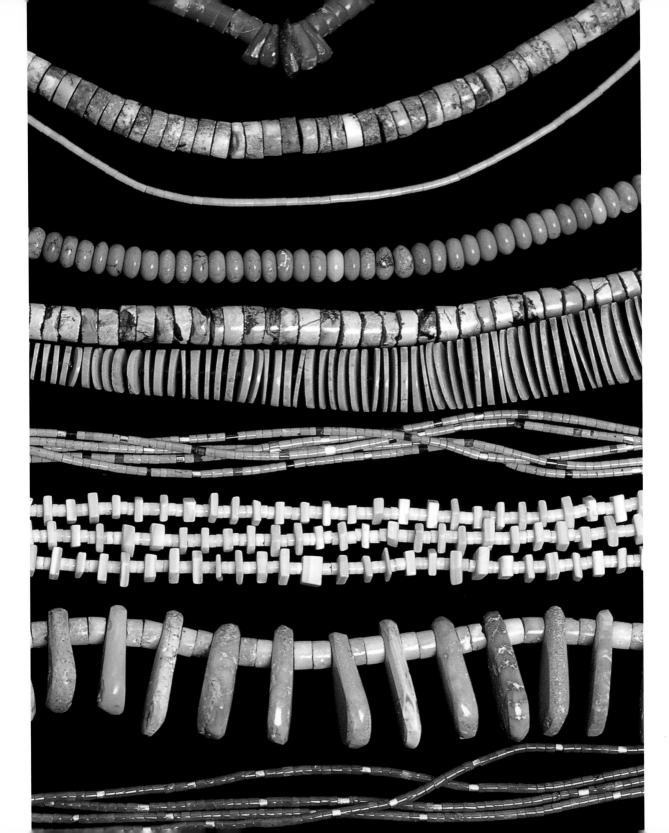

The careful reader will notice that, while the copy talks of Native Americans, it does not say the necklace is made by Indians. Nor does it say it was *handmade* (which means that every part was made by hand). It does say the cabochons were "hand set" and "hand polished," giving a careless reader the impression of authenticity. But all it really says is that someone (not necessarily a Southwestern Indian) probably put each one of these necklaces together from machine-cut cabochons and machine-made findings.

Also, if the turquoise were truly the Kingman mine's "finest," it would be gem quality or at least natural. And if it were gem quality or natural, the catalog would have said so directly. So one can assume that it is not the mine's "finest," but a lower grade. Again, if you love such a piece, by all means buy it, but be certain that you know exactly what you are getting. In buying Indian jewelry (as in most everything else), the advice of Tom Baker, owner of the Tanner Chaney Gallery in Albuquerque, is to "buy the best within the range that you can afford." He adds that for him "the hunt is where the fun is." In hunting for the best Indian jewelry in your price range, there are four basic criteria to keep in mind.

1. **Construction.** Is the piece solid, strong? This is relative, of course, for some jewelry is simply more delicate. For example, Navajos tend to prefer heavier, more solid pieces, while Zuni jewelry tends to be more delicate.
2. **Joints.** Where joints are soldered together, the soldering should not be visible. Joining parts invisibly is especially difficult for the artisan making a large piece.

Beaded necklaces by various artists including Ray Lovato and Percy Reano, Santo Domingo.

3. **Overall design.** Is it pleasing? Is the design clean, with color combinations you find attractive? (Baker emphasizes that in design "more is not always better.")
4. **Materials.** Silver jewelry should be silver, of course, but one does occasionally find it made from nickel-silver alloys. Indian jewelers now use a host of materials, including gold, and a large variety of stones. The stone most associated with Indian jewelry, however, is turquoise.

TURQUOISE

Like many valuable minerals, turquoise is a kind of miracle—the right elements in the right place over the right period of time and under the right conditions. It typically occurs in arid lands and usually in association with large amounts of its most important ingredient, copper. Technically it is a hydrated aluminum and copper phosphate, coming into being usually in the interstices of old metamorphic rock like granite when just the right amount of water percolates down from the surface of the land, carrying dissolved particles of aluminum and copper. It is copper that gives it its blue color, though an Indian legend says the color is stolen from the sky. The greener it is, the more iron it contains.

Water is also crucial to its color. When taken in chunks from the ground it will be bluish, but in the air, the water evaporates, leaving the softer, more porous turquoise increasingly pale.

In many galleries, stores, and other public places in the Southwest, one sees maps of Arizona, New Mexico, Colorado, and Nevada ringed with different chunks of turquoise, each with a line drawn to the location of one of the fabled turquoise mines of the American Southwest. In fact, so various is the output of each turquoise mine that virtually any natural turquoise you find could come from

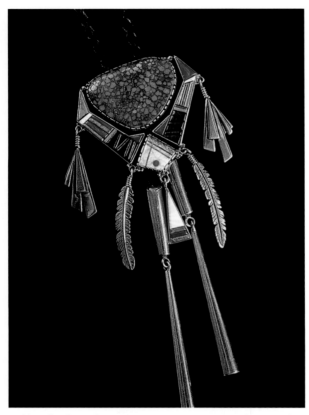

Gold pendant by Boyd Tsosie (Navajo), using turquoise, coral, ironwood, and fossilized ivory.

Turquoise is an almost wholly market-driven product. Today most turquoise used in Indian jewelry is imported from China, where it is plentiful and labor is cheap. Most Chinese turquoise appears to come from one place, but whatever name is suggested is a generic term that does not refer to a specific mine but simply means it is Chinese.

Most turquoise also has other elements in it, which show up as darker or lighter lines or squiggles. This is called *matrix*. Turquoise forms in association with surrounding rock, and this is often present in the final stone—it may be black, brown, golden, red. Often, the matrix forms distinct patterns, the rarest of which is called *spiderweb* and resembles a fine netting. Less than 1 percent of turquoise mined has spiderweb matrix.

Gallery owner Tom Baker points out that most Americans prefer turquoise with plenty of matrix, perhaps because it gives each stone a highly individual look, whereas visitors from abroad, especially Europe, prefer turquoise that is free of matrix and uniform in color. You can usually feel the matrix in the surface of a turquoise stone when you rub it gently with your finger.

GRADES OF TURQUOISE

The finest turquoise is called *gem quality*—meaning that it is of a gemlike hardness, which in turn means that it has few pores. The hardness is measured on the Mohs scale and gem quality is anything harder than 4.5 to 5.0 (though purists say it should be 5.5 or harder). Only 10 percent of the turquoise mined is of gem quality. Gem-quality precious stones—diamonds, emeralds, rubies, and so forth—are far more common.

Natural turquoise is the next level down in value, less hard than gem quality but hard enough to be used as it is.

virtually any mine. Even an expert can guess wrong from time to time. If you see turquoise you like, ask where it came from, and if it is "typical" of a particular mine, you may get the right answer.

One hears that the American turquoise mines are mostly played out now, but this is not exactly true. There is still a good deal of turquoise in the ground, but the mining companies now find it economical to use their equipment and capital to mine more expensive materials, such as gold. Federal mining regulations, which require heavy equipment for many parts of the mining process, have made mining turquoise unprofitable.

One is warned to keep such a stone away from hand lotion and other oils that may seep into its pores and change its color. On the other hand, just the normal oils from one's skin will do the same thing, and many like the look of old turquoise, its color altered and even enriched from wear. Some pieces have differentiated colors because of the different degrees of hardness of the individual stones used, giving the piece what some think a richer, more interesting look.

Stabilized turquoise: much of the turquoise mined is highly porous and turns white in the drying atmosphere. It is called *chalk,* and some of it is literally usable as chalk. But *stabilized* with clear plastic resin and high pressure, this low-grade turquoise can emerge bright blue or green and is virtually indistinguishable from higher-grade natural turquoise. The stabilization is permanent; such turquoise will not change color with age and use. Many of the finest artists use stabilized turquoise, and it is allowed under the stringent rules of the Indian Arts and Crafts Association. It is also possible to dye turquoise to give it a deeper color, but use of such stones, called *treated turquoise,* is *not* allowed by the IACA.

Large stones are stabilized in this manner. Other turquoise is *reconstituted,* meaning that tiny chips are mixed with epoxy and put under high pressure to create nicely colored, jewelry-size chunks. This is also permanent and is lower in rank than stabilized turquoise.

Block: regrettably, plastic imitation turquoise can be found in great quantity, sometimes with matrix-like designs added. (To the sharp-eyed, such phony matrix appears painted on.) This material is sold in supply stores in large blocks that look like huge oblong pieces of light-blue cheese. It is much easier to work with than natural turquoise, being of uniform hardness.

Block is easily scratched and in due course it will lose its luster, fade, even melt. To a minimally practiced eye it simply doesn't look real. Unscrupulous dealers (and artisans) will attempt to pass it off as real, however, even though that is against federal and most state law. Price is another indicator of turquoise quality: if the piece is on sale (often from a street vendor or souvenir store) for an oddly low price, it is probably plastic in machine-made settings. The buyer should always ask about the stone—is it natural, stabilized, treated, or block (plastic)? A false answer can leave a seller open to prosecution, so he or she is likely to reply either honestly or with a hedge.

A word of caution: the old test—stick a hot needle into the stone and if it melts, it's plastic—should not be attempted. Such an attack on a piece of *real* turquoise will cause it to crack and, in such cases, the rule usually is "You break it, you buy it."

Mosaic inlaid earrings with turquoise, coral, shell, and mother-of-pearl, by Ronald Chavez, Santo Domingo.

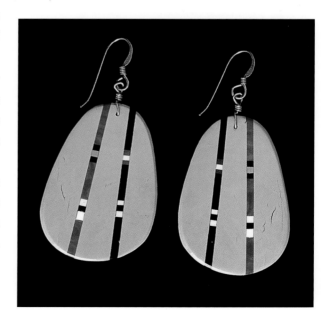

BEADS AND MOSAIC: SANTO DOMINGO

The pueblo of Santo Domingo continues the grand tradition of making jewelry in the manner of the ancestral people of the region, the Anasazi—in particular, making beads for beaded necklaces and other uses, and mosaic. Santo Domingo jewelers have long supplied other people of the region with beaded necklaces used for ceremonial and other purposes, and their work is widely available in stores and at special events.

Read more about Santo Domingo culture in the Pottery chapter (page 78).

Depression-era necklace, made from a red toothbrush handle and black material from a car battery; artist unknown, Santo Domingo.

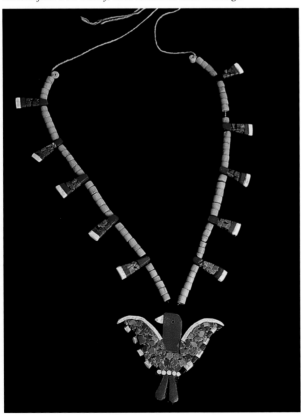

BEADWORK

Disk-shaped beads, ranging from small to tiny and made from a variety of materials—especially shell, turquoise, jet, coral, and ivory—remain popular favorites. They are cut, drilled with an electric drill (or very rarely a pump drill), strung (often on wire), and shaped by rolling them against sandstone slabs. (Some jewelers use modern lapidary equipment—power saws, drills, and sanders.) They will then be strung by the hundreds, even thousands, on music wire, fishing line, or fine silver chain.

Heishi is a Santo Domingo word that denotes fine disk beads made of shell, but the word is often improperly applied to all fine disk beadwork. Heishi, and similar fine beadwork in other materials, particularly turquoise and coral, which came into use only in the twentieth century, may be strung on single or multiple strands. Clasps may be silver findings or wrapped with fine, white string to make a traditional *cotton wrap,* or a single strand of tied string. The latter two clasp styles are often preferred by Indian people for ceremonial necklaces.

Such a necklace may also have another smaller loop or two, called *joclas,* hanging from it like a pendant. *Jocla* is a Navajo-derived word for ear, and these smaller "necklaces" are traditionally earrings, and tied to necklaces when not worn as such.

As noted earlier, real heishi is one of the hardest to find of jewelry components, and the market is flooded with foreign-made machine-cut versions. Real heishi, experts point out, feels like liquid flowing in your hand; imitation heishi doesn't. And certain stones, like lapis lazuli, are not suitable for making heishi. A string of "lapis heishi" is made from block, or plastic.

Because fewer and fewer artisans are making authentic heishi, and more are replacing them with machine-made beads, experts consider real heishi an excellent investment.

Larger, flat beads called *tabs* are combined with heishi-type beads to make *bead-and-tab* necklaces; you may also find raw chunks of turquoise interpolated among smaller beads. To such necklaces, pendants of various types can also be added.

Santo Domingo lapidarists have long supplied Zuni craftsmen with heishi and heishi-style beadwork, to which the Zunis add small, hand-carved animal fetishes—either all the same, such as bears or birds, or a variety of animal types.

Yet another type of necklace is made up of an eclectic variety of precious found objects. Called *grandmother necklaces,* these are based on the notion of an old grandmother happily picking up small bits and pieces of things from here and there on the ground as she walks along.

MOSAIC

A revival in the ancient craft of mosaic began in the early 1970s through the work of one woman, Angie Reano Owen of Santo Domingo, who researched the old Hohokam style of adding shaped pieces of turquoise and other stones to Glycymeris bracelets and other shell objects. She used traditional materials for all of it, except for using epoxy dyed black instead of pine pitch as glue. One Reano innovation among many was the *chiclet* necklace: strands of beads incorporating small cubes with mosaic on all sides. Reano also supplied shells decorated with mosaic for ceremonial purposes in the pueblo.

The new/old style of mosaic quickly caught on in the market and among Angie Reano Owen's brothers Percy and Frank, and their wives, Charlotte and Charlene

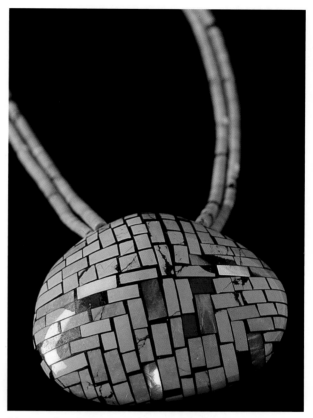

Mosaic pendant of turquoise, coral, lapis, and mother-of-pearl affixed to a shell, on a strand of handmade turquoise beads, by Charlene Sanchez Reano, Santo Domingo.

Sanchez, and other jewelers. They have adapted mosaic to a wide variety of jewelry types—seashell pendants for heishi-style necklaces, bracelets of many kinds, earrings, hair pieces, and so forth. Yet other artists combine mosaic designs with silver to create earrings, belt buckles, bolos (also sometimes called "bolas"), and necklace pendants. Charlene Sanchez Reano, of San Felipe, and her Santo Domingo husband, Frank, have recently created a reversible inlay necklace that has won virtually every artistic award and has given them international recognition and gallery shows.

NAVAJO SILVER AND STONES

Iron- and silversmithing were introduced into the Southwest by the Spaniards, but it was not until the middle of the nineteenth century that the Navajos in particular began to make silver jewelry. Prior to this, Southwestern Indians, and particularly Navajos, used copper for adornment and to "frame" pieces of turquoise. Navajos carried a piece of turquoise in a medicine pouch for its healing and protective powers (it also brings strength), and considered it bad luck not to have it. With the advent of silversmithing, it was possible to wear the turquoise. A major Navajo tradition is to use the metal as a kind of sculpture to frame a whole stone.

The first Navajo silversmith, Atsidi Sani, went on to teach his four sons. At first melted coinage was hammered into various shapes and decorated by means of cold chisels,

Concha belt by Herman Charley, Navajo.

files, and stamps. Another early technique was sand-casting, in which molten silver was poured into a hand-carved stone mold. Yet another casting material was tufa, a fine-grained, compacted volcanic ash. In those days, the jeweler provided heat by means of a fire and bellows.

An early product was the *concha belt* (also sometimes incorrectly called "concho" belt), consisting of a number of similar oval silver disks, stamped with designs and hammered into a convex shape, and worn on a belt. The concha was a Plains Indian tradition (copper and brass ovals were previously used to fasten the sides of buckskin leggings, and Navajos traded so-called chief blankets to the Plains tribes for them). The scalloped edges were a Navajo adaptation of a Mexican design.

A popular necklace form was the *squash blossom,* consisting of a double-crescent silver pendant ending in stylized "hands" and smaller silver beads similarly shaped.

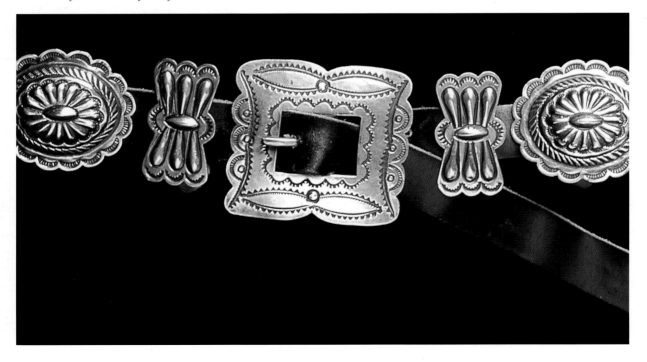

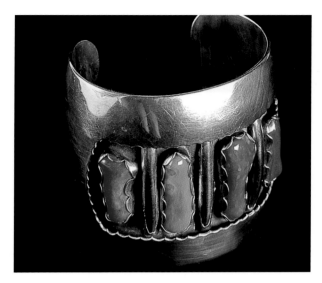

Heavy silver bracelet with coral mounted in "shadow boxes," by Thompson Piaso, Navajo.

The origin of "squash blossom" is unknown: the term may derive from the pomegranate fruit, a favored Mexican design element of the period. The Navajo word for this kind of necklace means "beads that spread out."

An early Pueblo variation on the squash blossom necklace—perhaps Isletan in origin—was the *cross* necklace, in which silver crosses were substituted for or added to the pendant and beads.

During the nineteenth century, Navajo jewelers made a variety of relatively simple rings, bracelets, earrings (for example, a loop of silver through a drilled bead), buttons and blouse ornaments for women, and bow guards (often an oval silver piece mounted on leather, originally to protect the wrist from a snapping bowstring, and adapted for a variety of ceremonial purposes) for men, as well as decorations for their horses' bridles. Jewelry was an important sign of prestige and wealth, served as items for barter with local traders and others, and was widely traded by Navajos to other tribes in the region.

The tradition of *pawn* came into being with the advent of Navajo jewelry. A family might trade jewelry for various items (food, etc.) from the local trader during the year, redeeming it with cash earned from the trader for the sale of lambs or wool or rugs. Typically, such jewelry was kept on display in the trading post so the Navajos would know it was still there, awaiting the lambing or shearing season, and honest traders sold it only after the owner moved away or died. Once widely available, pawn is now relatively scarce, though it may turn up in the sale of older collections.

It was only in the 1880s that Navajo jewelers mastered soldering and began cutting and shaping turquoise stones and setting them in silver. More often than not, a single stone, often quite large, would be set in the center of a concha or other silver piece.

Silversmithing and turquoise soon spread to Zuni and elsewhere, and a Zuni-originated style of bracelet soon became popular among Navajo jewelers: the *cluster*

Bow guard with silver stamping and turquoise, by Wayne Aguilar, Navajo.

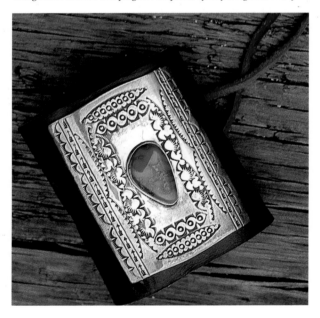

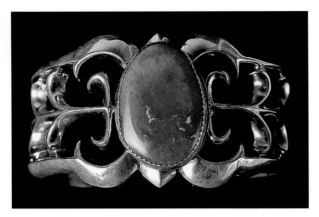

Old-style silver and turquoise bracelet by Wilfred Henry, Navajo.

Navajo tendency toward the bold and dramatic use of stones framed in a metal sculpture, a style now freely adopted and adapted by jewelers of many other tribes as well. Navajo jewelers (and other Indians working in a Navajo-like style) have greatly expanded the range of materials and design of jewelry.

Read more about Navajo culture in the Weaving chapter (page 33).

ZUNI SILVER AND STONES

In 1872 a Zuni named Lanyade learned silversmithing from a Navajo craftsman, and for two decades Zuni jewelry followed the style and technique of the Navajos. In the 1890s, however, Zunis learned the art of setting turquoise and developed a wholly different tradition.

In general, Zuni jewelers saw silver as secondary in importance, a means of holding turquoise in place. They followed the lead of Mexican jewelers, using filigree and

Silver and needlepoint turquoise squash blossom by Victoria Naha, Zuni.

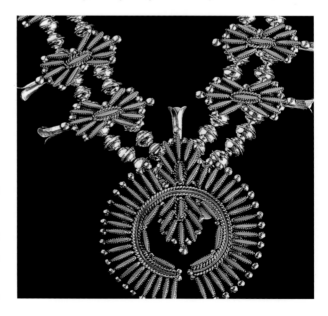

bracelet, in which a number of cut turquoise stones were set in silver around a larger central one. Similar clusters would adorn bow guards and other items. More recently, Navajos have also borrowed the Zuni technique of inlay, adapting it to their own tastes and cultural meanings and symbols (and typically preferring it to be heavier than Zuni inlay).

In the early twentieth century, tourism encouraged the sale of Indian jewelry to the point where cheap items were cranked out in what amounted to sweatshops in Albuquerque and elsewhere, often with thin sheets of silver—or even nickel, used as a substitute—along with cheap turquoise substitutes. But in the 1940s and particularly after World War II, various Indian and non-Indian organizations began encouraging the return to the traditional craftsmanship and styles. This, plus the introduction of electrical equipment and many finer kinds of tools, along with the addition of new materials such as coral and other stones besides turquoise, led to a flowering of silversmithery and other forms among Navajos and other Southwestern tribal people. Even in its most modern form, as craft has become art, there is a recognizable dangles, fine wire and small bezels, and set multiple stones in elaborate patterns. This was in clear contrast to the heavier Navajo jewelry, in which often broad areas of silver set off larger stones. As noted above, the "cluster" style then passed back to Navajos, but never in the elaborate Zuni style of using multiple small stones—sometimes up to 150 or so in a single bracelet.

From cluster bracelets, even more elaborate styles evolved—*petit point,* featuring great quantities of tiny teardrop-shaped or oval stones, and *needlepoint,* in which

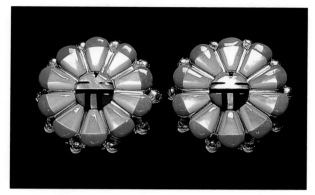

Sun-face cuff links with turquoise and mother-of-pearl inlaid in gold, by Mike Simplicio, Zuni.

Gambel's quail inlaid in a silver pendant with silver beads, by an unknown Zuni artist, 1950s (before use of tortoise shell became illegal with passage of the Endangered Species Act).

the stones are pointed at both ends. Petit point and needlepoint are widely used in pins, bracelets, earrings, and other items.

Zuni jewelry soon became so popular that most of the tribal members were engaged in making it to the exclusion of making pottery, which brought less income for comparable time. A tradition of carefully observing the work of others is still in place at Zuni, a kind of tribal quality control.

Read more about Zuni culture in the Carvings chapter (page 42).

Channel inlay bracelet, Zuni.

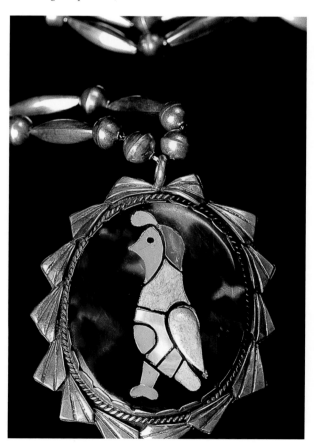

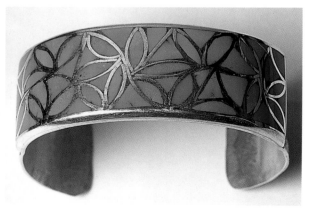

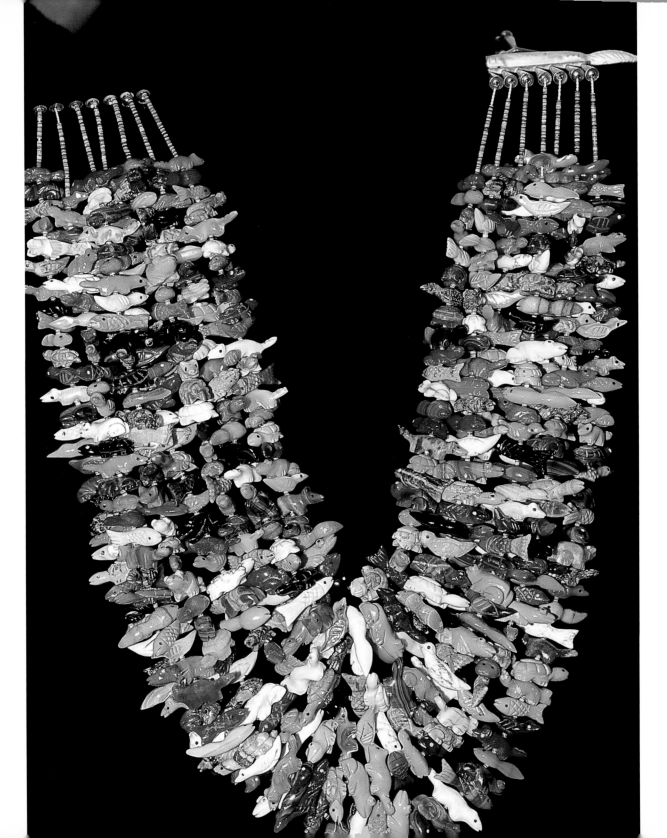

ZUNI CHANNEL INLAY

In the 1940s, another Zuni tradition began: *channel inlay.* Thin strips of silver are soldered to a silver plate, forming

LEFT: Elaborate fetish necklace by Dinah and Pete Gaspar, Zuni.
BELOW: Fossilized ivory fetish necklace by Lena Boone, Zuni.

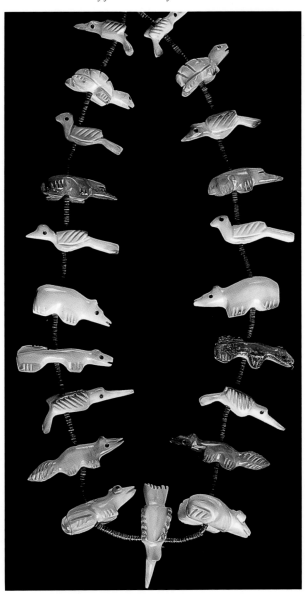

cells in which carefully cut pieces of stone and shell are cemented to form a particular design. Then the entire piece is ground down to a smooth surface.

Typical designs are naturalistic birds (like the cardinal), butterflies, and flowers, but they also include representational figures (like clowns), and straightforward geometric designs. Unlike mosaic (which Zuni jewelers also use), in channel inlay the silver dividers show and are part of the design. This technique has been used in a variety of pieces from pins to concha belts.

FETISH NECKLACES

In the 1940s, a Zuni carver named Leekya Deyuse began carving small fetish-type animals that were strung on heishi necklaces. The new concept caught on quickly with other jewelers and carvers—and with the public—and fetish necklaces are now among the most popular forms of Southwestern Indian jewelry. They are made in single and multiple strands, on heishi or with larger beads. Some will feature a single animal such as bears or birds; others will be a complete Zuni bestiary. All kinds of material are used for the carvings, from turquoise, coral, jet, and local stones such as pipestone, to exotic materials such as fossil ivory and imported marble.

HOPI SILVER OVERLAY

Until World War II, the few Hopi who made silver jewelry followed the lead of the Navajo silversmiths in the surrounding area. Then, in a project sponsored by Harold and Mary-Russell Colton of the Museum of Northern Arizona, a new Hopi style emerged. The Coltons researched old Hopi design elements, mostly those that had been rediscovered for pottery. The intricacy of the designs called for different techniques, and after the war,

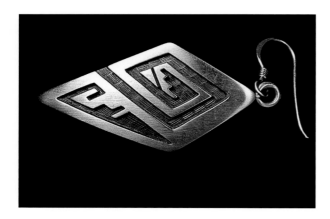

Earring by Pat Tewawina, Hopi.

several veterans—including Hopi artist Fred Kabotie—devised the style called *Hopi overlay*.

Pendant by Farron Joseyesva, Hopi.

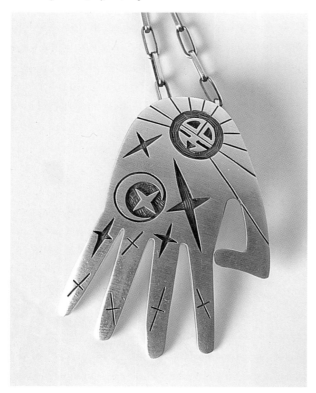

A design is carefully sawed out of a flat piece of silver (say, for a bracelet). This piece with the cut-out is then soldered to another piece of approximately the same size and shape. The design-bearing side is then oxidized, turning it black, and polished to either a shiny or matte finish, leaving the cutout design black. Typically, the cutout design will first be precisely hand-stamped to give it texture as well, and a sign of excellence is the fineness of this stamping. Another important sign of excellent workmanship, of course, is the precision of the sawing.

Yet another sign of quality is the weight of the silver used, as Alph Secakuku, owner of Hopi Fine Arts on Second Mesa, Arizona, explains. As noted, an overlay piece is made from two pieces, a slightly thicker one in which the design is cut out, soldered to a thinner one. The thickness of the sheets is graded on a scale in which the lower the number, the thicker the sheet. The seller may be able to tell you that a bracelet is 18 over 20, meaning that both pieces are *relatively* thin. A 16 over 20 would be thicker, and 14 or 16 over 18 thicker still and more costly. One can sense these variations simply by picking up two pieces and comparing their heft. Thicker (heavier) is better.

Belt buckle by Chalmers Day, Hopi.

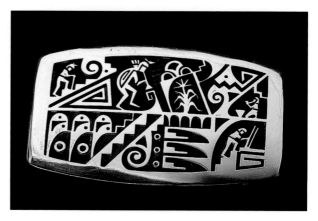

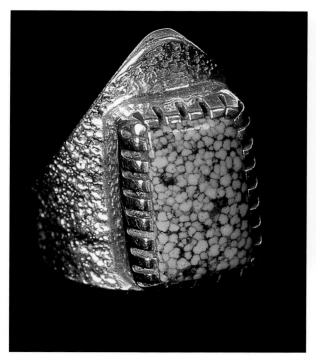

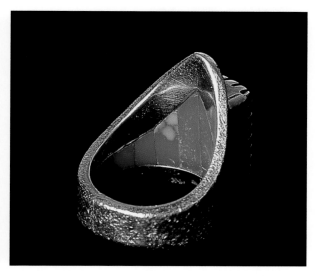

ABOVE & ABOVE RIGHT: Gold ring by Charles Loloma, Hopi, with stones inlaid on the inside as well as mounted on the outer surface.

Hopi overlay traditionally resulted in elegant jewelry that was both simple *and* bold, and the new style flourished. Hopi jewelers made bracelets, conchas, pins, rings, earrings, and other forms with designs of varying complexity. Frequently used design elements were bear paws and various abstract representations of lightning, corn, and moisture, along with the Hopi sun and favorite animals such as lizards and birds.

In the early years, turquoise and other stones were rarely added, though this began to change in the 1970s. Even so, Hopi jewelry tended to be comparatively expensive, owing in part to the fact that there were simply fewer jewelers than in other tribes.

Read more about Hopi culture in the Carvings chapter (pages 48–49).

NEW DIRECTIONS

As the years progressed, styles began to be passed back and forth among the tribes, and new ideas, materials, and techniques were incorporated. But it was a Hopi jeweler named Charles Loloma who can be credited with bringing

Gold bracelet by Verma Nequatewa, Hopi, who apprenticed with her famous uncle, Charles Loloma.

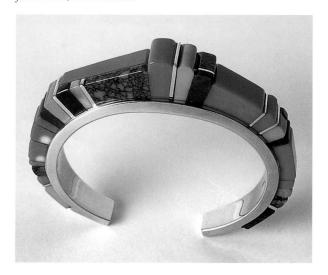

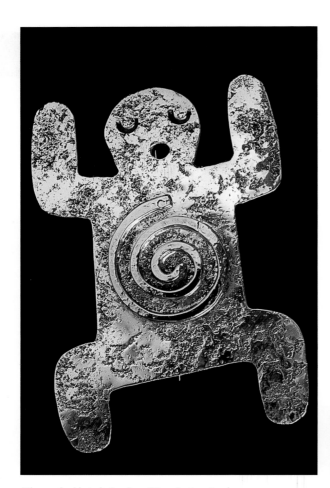

Silver and gold pin by Jan Loco, Warm Springs Apache.

worldwide. Its effect on Southwestern Indian and other Indian jewelers was profound. Some were influenced to the point of imitation, but for others, his innovative approach opened the door to a variety of new interpretations of tribal traditions and values.

Of course, jewelry-making is not restricted to a few tribes. The ones featured here have the longest and most distinct traditions in this art. For example, the Tohono O'odham numbered a few silversmiths over the decades, but these tended to follow the Navajo style, as did the Hopi until the mid-twentieth century. Now several young O'odham silversmiths are striking out on their own and in a style more reminiscent of Hopi overlay. Others, like the Apache jeweler whose piece is shown here, while mindful of ancient designs and meanings, are seeking a wholly personal style and expression.

Silver overlay buckle with Man-in-the-Maze design, by James Fendenheim, Tohono O'odham.

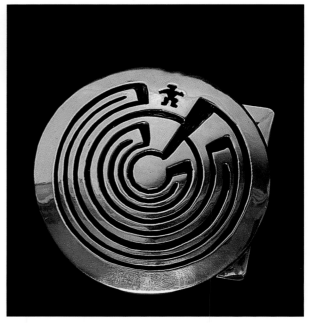

about a major revolution in Indian jewelry in general (and other associated art forms). After starting out (unusual for a Hopi man) as a potter, Loloma began making jewelry in the 1950s. He used new materials—ironwood, lapis lazuli, malachite, fossilized ivory, coral—and created wholly new designs. His "height bracelets," with stones set as slabs of varying height, suggested the Southwestern landscape. He also took to inlaying stones on the *inside* of bracelets and rings, as a reflection of the wearer's spirit and private self. Loloma's innovative work was soon known

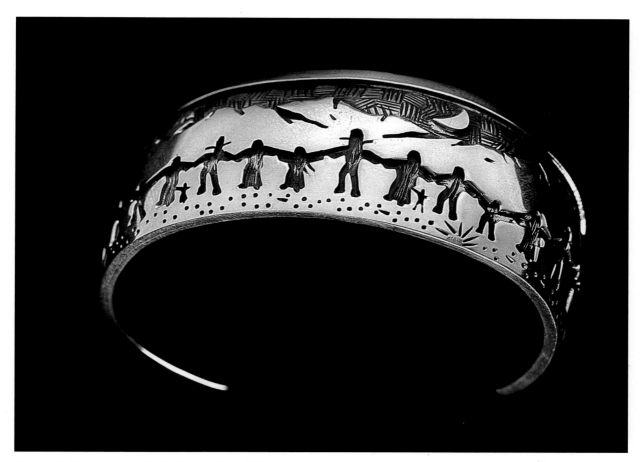

Silver overlay friendship bracelet by Rick Manuel, Tohono O'odham.

While much traditional Southwestern Indian jewelry is being made today, much of it is verging into the realm of fine art.

CHAPTER SEVEN

VISITING THE INDIAN VILLAGES

MANY OF THE PUEBLO TRIBES have found it necessary to erect signs outside their villages requesting that visitors neither photograph, sketch, nor record anything on their land. They enforce these rules vigorously. At Taos and a few others, permits can be obtained. This is not, for the most part, a concern that one's soul might be captured and taken away on film, as with some tribal people; almost any Pueblo home contains photographs of family members, particularly those who are veterans of the U.S. armed services. It is simply a matter of privacy. If a pueblo

(or any reservation) has not posted explicit notices, the prudent and courteous thing to do is to leave your camera in the car and ask. At the end of each tribal capsule history in this section are the telephone numbers you can call to inquire about rules for taking pictures.

Unless it is otherwise noted, the Pueblos neither welcome nor prohibit driving through "to get a look at a Pueblo," but such rubbernecking is looked upon with the same enthusiasm it would be by any out-of-the-way village dweller in any society. At the same time, some

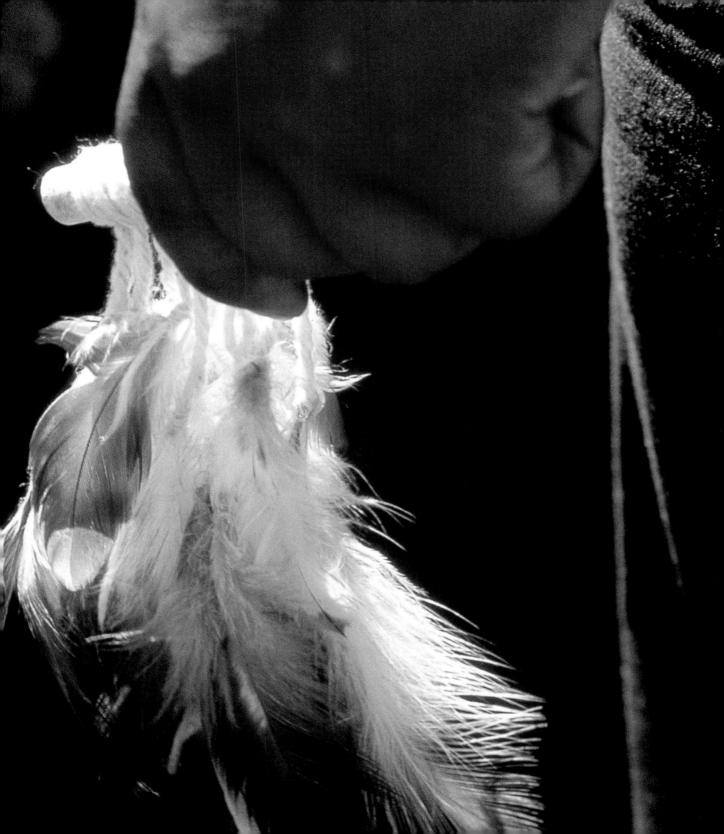

pueblo residents sell crafts out of their homes, with signs to that effect.

Several of the pueblos hold ceremonies at various times of year that are open to the public. These are religious ceremonies first and foremost, and non-Indians as well as Indians of other tribes are sometimes welcome, on the premise that the more people joining in the prayers, the more effective the prayers and the ceremony will be. Again, one can call in advance.

A rule of thumb for non-Indian outsiders visiting such a ceremony and trying to find a place to see the proceedings is *always* to take a back seat (or back row) to Indian people trying to do the same. A visitor will often see people clambering onto houses to see the ceremony from the roof: if invited onto the roof, accept; otherwise, it is courteous to remain on the ground.

The following capsule sketches of the twenty Pueblo groups are organized geographically, moving from west to east to northeast, and followed by other Southwest tribes .

VISITING HOPI. State Route 264 winds from Keams Canyon (seat of the Bureau of Indian Affairs agency for the tribe) through the center of Hopi, alongside or over the three mesas, and all the way to Moenkopi (near Tuba City). All the villages are reached from this highway.

In addition to the Hopi Cultural Center complex, which includes a museum and a motel, and the nearby Hopi Arts and Crafts Guild, there are a number of individual galleries and shops set up by Hopi artisans, mostly along or within sight of Route 264, or with signs directing visitors into specific villages.

Katsina dances take place in one village or another during almost every weekend from early June through July. Some of these dances are open to outsiders, but whether or not a dance is open varies from village to village and year to year. A decision to close a dance is arrived at only painfully by the kiva leader in charge, almost always the result of rudeness or other misbehavior in a previous year. Information about what dances are open to the public can be obtained from the Hopi Cultural Center (928-734-2401) or the tribal government's Office of Public Relations in Kykotsmovi (928-734-3000; P.O. Box 123, Kykotsmovi, AZ 86039). Helpful information can be found for all Arizona tribes at Intertribal Council of Arizona's website: www.itcaonline.com.

VISITING ZUNI. The village of Zuni lies along state Route 53, a few miles west of the turnoff from Route 602 that leads south from Gallup.

Two Zuni-owned places to obtain crafts are: Pueblo of Zuni Arts and Crafts (505-782-5531; 1222 State Highway 53, Zuni, NM 87327) and Zuni Craftsmen Cooperative Association (505-782-4425; 1177 State Highway 53, Zuni, NM 87327). There are a number of other retail establishments (not Indian-owned), including Pueblo Trading Post and Turquoise Village, in and outside the village that have excellent wares as well.

VISITING ACOMA. Highway signs on U.S. Route 40 point the way to "Sky City," some fourteen miles south of the highway. Below it there is the Sky City Visitor Center and Museum, from which guided tours of the high pueblo are conducted (for a fee) throughout most of the year (505-470-4966 or 800-747-0181). The Center has been beautifully rebuilt after a tragic fire burnt it down, along with a host of valuable artifacts and art. Crafts are for sale at the center, which houses a museum with exhibits on pottery and history. Pottery is also on sale at

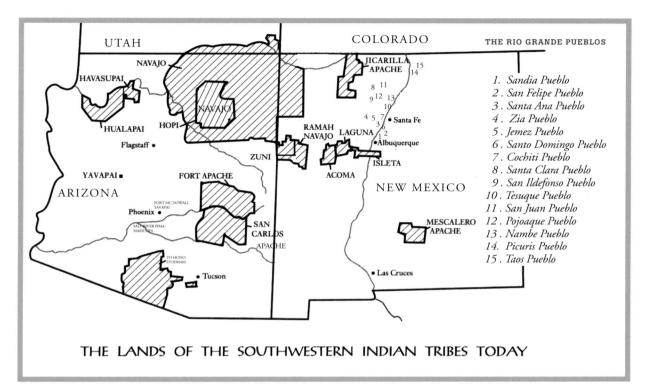

THE LANDS OF THE SOUTHWESTERN INDIAN TRIBES TODAY

THE RIO GRANDE PUEBLOS

1. Sandia Pueblo
2. San Felipe Pueblo
3. Santa Ana Pueblo
4. Zia Pueblo
5. Jemez Pueblo
6. Santo Domingo Pueblo
7. Cochiti Pueblo
8. Santa Clara Pueblo
9. San Ildefonso Pueblo
10. Tesuque Pueblo
11. San Juan Pueblo
12. Pojoaque Pueblo
13. Nambe Pueblo
14. Picuris Pueblo
15. Taos Pueblo

stalls near the visitor center, and on top. Further information can be obtained from the Pueblo of Acoma (505-552-6604; P.O. Box 309, Acomita, NM 87034).

VISITING LAGUNA. Laguna pottery and other tribal crafts such as jewelry and belts are on sale by members of the village. Additional information, including about local artisans, can be obtained from the Pueblo of Laguna (505-552-6654; P.O. Box 194, Laguna, NM 87026, www.lagunaonline.org).

VISITING ISLETA. The pueblo is a few miles southwest of Isleta Lakes off Route 47, which is in turn thirteen miles south of Albuquerque on I-25. For further information contact the Pueblo of Isleta (505-869-3111; P.O. Box 1270, Isleta, NM 87022).

VISITING SANDIA. Tourists are not encouraged to visit this private place, but off Tramway Boulevard on the southern side of the reservation is the tribe's Bien Mur Indian Market Center (505-821-5400, www.benmuir.com), featuring crafts from a variety of tribal sources. For further information, contact the Sandia Pueblo (505-867-3317; P.O. Box 6008, Bernalillo, NM 87004).

VISITING SANTO DOMINGO. Midway between Albuquerque and Santa Fe on U.S. Route 25, state Route 22 leads east to the pueblo. During the public ceremonies at the pueblo, craftsmen and other vendors—only from other tribes—will have booths selling craft items and food. Parking at such events is provided by the pueblo in specified areas outside the village center but within easy walking distance of the festivities. People come and go throughout the day.

VISITING COCHITI. Cochiti Pueblo is reached by turning west off U.S. Route 25 onto state Route 22, which leads one past Santo Domingo and then the largely Hispanic farm town of Pena Blanca, or by turning west on state Route 16 (nearer to Santa Fe), which ends at Route 22 a couple of miles below the Cochiti dam. Information about local artisans can be found only by driving into the village and looking for signs.

VISITING SAN FELIPE. If one is driving in or near this pueblo, oncoming drivers lift their hands in a greeting wave—just a little piece of local manners. State Route 313, which goes through the largely Hispanic town of Algodones (itself some 15 miles north of Albuquerque), leads into San Felipe Pueblo, as does the pueblo's own turnoff from U.S. Route 25 some 4 miles north of the highway's Algodones turnoff. As at other pueblos along the Rio Grande, food and craft booths spring up during ceremonials.

VISITING SANTA ANA. The Ranchitos portion of Santa Ana and its various tribal enterprises are found by turning west off U.S. Route 25 onto state Route 44 to the west side of the Rio Grande. Arts and crafts are available at the Ta Ma Ya (55 Dove Road). For further information, contact Santa Ana Pueblo (505-867-3301, Bernalillo, NM 87004, www.santaana.org).

VISITING ZIA. Zia Pueblo is reached by turning off state Route 44 some sixteen miles northeast of U.S. Route 25. Pottery and other crafts (and pottery demonstrations) are available weekdays at the Zia Cultural Center (135 Capitol Square Drive). For further information contact Zia Pueblo (505-867-3304; San Ysidro, NM 87053).

VISITING JEMEZ. Jemez is located on Route 4, off Route 44 some forty miles northwest of Bernalillo. Information and crafts are available at the Jemez Visitor Center. For further information, contact Pueblo of Jemez (505-834-7235; P.O. Box 100, Jemez Pueblo, NM 87024).

VISITING SANTA CLARA. The pueblo is located two miles south of Española on Route 30 to Los Alamos. In the village are many shops and homes selling crafts (look for signs out front). For further information, including that on guided tours and other recreational activities on the reservation, contact Santa Clara Pueblo (505-753-7326; P.O. Box 580, Española, NM 87532).

VISITING SAN ILDEFONSO. Take Route 84 north from Santa Fe, turn off at Pojoaque on Route 502 to Los Alamos, and turn right after about eight miles. In the village, signs indicate homes and workshops where crafts are for sale. Permits are available on-site for fishing and picnicking along the Rio Grande. The January 23 feast day starts with a dawn Animal Dance. Crafts are also available at the Visitor and Information Center (505-455-3549). There is a Maria Poveka Martinez Museum and also the San Ildefonso museum. For further information, contact San Ildefonso Pueblo (505-455-2273; Route 5, Santa Fe, NM 87501).

VISITING TESUQUE. Tesuque is located nine miles north of Santa Fe on U.S. Route 84. Tesuque Pueblo Flea Market, on Opera Hill off Interstate 84/285 near Santa Fe, is open every weekend between February and December. There are more than 1,200 booths. For information about local craftspeople (particularly potters), contact Tesuque Pueblo (505-983-2667; Route 5, Box 360T, Santa Fe, NM 87501).

VISITING NAMBE. To reach Nambe, drive north on U.S. Route 84 to twenty miles north of Santa Fe; turn right on Route 503, then travel six miles east to the sign that reads "Nambe Falls," and three more miles to the pueblo entrance. Some crafts are available in local stores and homes. For further information, contact Nambe Pueblo (505-455-2036; Rural Route 1, Box 117-BB, Santa Fe, NM 87501).

VISITING POJOAQUE. The pueblo is fifteen miles north of Santa Fe on U.S. Route 84. For further information, contact the Pueblo of Pojoaque (505-455-2278; 39 Camino de Rincon, Santa Fe, NM 87506).

VISITING SAN JUAN. San Juan (also known as Ohkay Owingeh) is located about a mile north of Española, off Route 68. There are a number of crafts shops in the pueblo itself, and local artisans are well represented at the O'ke Oweenge Crafts Cooperative, open Monday through Saturday (505-852-2372). For further information contact San Juan Pueblo (505-852-4400; P.O. Box 1099, San Juan Pueblo, NM 87566).

VISITING PICURIS. The pueblo is located between Taos and Santa Fe, seven miles northwest of the town of Peñasco on Route 75. The pueblo's visitor center includes a museum (505-587-2957) that sells local arts and crafts, particularly pottery, and pottery is sold from homes as well. Camera permits are available. For further information, contact Picuris Pueblo (505-587-2519; P.O. Box 127, Peñasco, NM 87553).

VISITING TAOS. Taos Pueblo, which charges an admission and parking fee, is located about two miles northeast of the Taos, New Mexico, plaza. Written permission is required for sketching, painting, or commercial photography; no cameras or recording devices are allowed at any ceremonies. The pueblo is closed on San Geronimo's feast day, September 30, and visitors are asked to respect off-limit signs and not to climb any of the ladders outside the homes. On the road leading in are various crafts stores.

VISITING HAVASUPAI. Leaving Route 66 northwest of Seligman, Arizona, Indian Service Road 18 ends at Hualapai Hilltop, the staging area for hikers and pack trains heading for Supai Village. This is a nine-mile trip, including a 1,000-foot descent that is not for acrophobes. Reservations for horse transport and the tribal motel and campgrounds should be made well in advance and confirmed by calling the Havasupai Tourism Office (928-448-2121; Supai, AZ 86435). In addition to the motel, you'll find a cafe and a general store/trading post where basketry and beadwork are sold. The main attractions in the canyon are the spectacular falls: Havasu, Mooney, and Beaver.

VISITING HUALAPAI. Visitors wishing to travel off state Route 66 on the reservation need to acquire a permit from tribal headquarters in Peach Springs. Contact Hualapai Tribal Council (928-769-2216; P.O. Box 179, Peach Springs, AZ 86434).

VISITING TOHONO O'ODHAM. Arts and crafts (including Tohono O'odham basketry) are available from vendors near the stunning church of San Xavier del Bac, nine miles southwest of Tucson off Mission Road just off I-19 (520-294-2624). They are also available at the celebration called the O'odham Tash at Casa Grande in February. For further information, contact Tohono O'odham (P.O. Box 837, Sells, AZ 85634; 520-383-2028).

VISITING SALT RIVER PIMA-MARICOPA. The Salt River Pima-Maricopa Indian Reservation (52,000 acres that are home to some 6,000 enrolled members who speak different languages but share cultural values) is just west of Scottsdale on McDowell Road. The Hoo-Hoogam Ki Museum (10005 E. Osborn Road, Scottsdale, AZ 85256, 480-850-8190) sells Pima basketry and Maricopa pottery. For more information, contact the tribe's community relations department (480-850-8000).

VISITING JICARILLA APACHES. In Dulce, the tribally operated Jicarilla Arts and Crafts Gift Shop (505-759-4274) displays and sells those traditional crafts still being practiced—chiefly basket making, plus beadwork and tanning buckskin; there is also a museum in the same building.

VISITING MESCALERO APACHES. The Mescalero Reservation lies northeast of Alamogordo, New Mexico, on U.S. Route 70. On the Fourth of July, the tribe holds a ceremony honoring young women who have come of age during the year, and this is accompanied by dances by the Mountain Spirits as well as rodeo and arts and crafts shows. For information, contact Mescalero Apache Nation (505-464-4494; P.O. Box 227, Mescalero, NM 88340).

VISITING WESTERN APACHES. Poverty has continued to be a problem among these people, but tribal income now comes from operating a year-round resort, Sunrise Park Resort, three miles south of McNary (928-735-7669, 800-772-7669), as well as the granting of hunting and fishing licenses in the still-untrammeled wildernesses of the northern reservation. For further information, contact San Carlos Reservation (928-475-2361; P.O. Box 1240, San Carlos, AZ 85550) and White Mountain Apache Tribal Headquarters (928-338-4346; P.O. Box 700, Whiteriver, AZ 85941).

VISITING THE NAVAJOS. Among the courtesies of Navajo culture you should observe, one is to remain in your car a few minutes outside a Navajo home if you have been invited there either personally or by a sign advertising crafts for sale. One does not simply drive up to a Navajo camp or other private Navajo residence. Also, as noted elsewhere, a Navajo handshake is soft and brief, and to look someone directly in the eye is considered a challenge, not a courtesy.

Lodging is available in the main population centers of Window Rock, Chinle, Kayenta, and Tuba City. In all, the reservation contains fifteen national monuments, tribal parks, and historic sites—including Monument Valley and Canyon de Chelly (pronounced de SHAY), two of the most strikingly beautiful landforms on the continent. Detailed information on lodging, recreation, and other tourist attractions is available from the Navajo Tourism Department. Throughout the reservation are trading posts and galleries where the wide range of Navajo arts and crafts can be seen and purchased. For further information, contact Navajo Tourism Department (928-871-6436; P.O. Box 663, Window Rock, AZ 86515, www.navajo.org).

VISITING THE SAN JUAN PAIUTES. The reservation around Hidden Springs is about twenty miles from Tuba City, Arizona, off U.S. Route 89 north of its junction with U.S. Route 160.

ACKNOWLEDGMENTS

Over the years, many Southwestern Indian craftspeople have made us welcome, taught us, and offered us the most priceless gift of all: friendship. Many of them have steered us to galleries and museum shops that are widely respected by both Indian craftspeople and collectors. Even though some people have moved on and a few establishments have regrouped or fallen by the wayside since we began our research many years ago, we remain indebted to the following individuals, galleries, museum shops, and other organizations:

Mark Bahti of Bahti Indian Arts in Tucson, Arizona, and Santa Fe, New Mexico; Lynn Bullock (and her superb library), James Barajas, and Byron Hunter of the Heard Museum Shop, Phoenix, Arizona; Dan Garland, Steve Mattoon, Tracy Watkins, Sandy Winborne, Mike Krajnak, and Betty Johnson of Garland's Navajo Rugs in Sedona, Arizona; Bill Garland, Susan Garland and Alan Grodzinsky and their daughter Sacha, Britt Burns, and Lynn Valeruz of Garland's Indian Jewelry, Sedona, Arizona; Ron Preston and Joseph and Janice Day of Tsakurshovi on Second Mesa, Arizona (originators of the now world-famous T-shirt "Don't Worry Be Hopi"); Verma Nequatewa and Bob Rhodes of Sonwai in Hotevilla, Arizona; Bruce McGee, Sylvia Clark, and Yvonne Baca of McGee's Native American Gallery in Holbrook, Arizona; Ron McGee, Verlinda Adams, and Nadine Lomawunu of McGee's Trading Post in Keams Canyon, Arizona; Anna Matson and Steven Pickle of the Museum of Northern Arizona Shop in Flagstaff, Arizona; Bill Malone and Sandra White; Phil Woodard of Indian Jewelry Supply in Gallup, New Mexico; Steve Draper of the former Pueblo and Plains (which has since merged with Adobe Gallery in Santa Fe) in Taos, New Mexico; Françoise Draper of Françoise in Taos, New Mexico; Tom and Laura Baker of Tanner Chaney Gallery in Albuquerque, New Mexico; Al Anthony, Ken Zintak, and Eric Sanchez of Adobe Gallery in Santa Fe, New Mexico; Karen McCartney of Native Gold, Albuquerque, New Mexico; David Guttierez of the Maxwell Museum Store, Albuquerque, New Mexico; Roger Smith of Palms Trading Company, Albuquerque, New Mexico; Rob Lucas of the Case Trading Post in the Wheelwright Museum of the American Indian, Santa Fe, New Mexico; the late Susan McGuire, executive director of the Indian Arts and Crafts Association in Albuquerque, New Mexico; Yin May-Lee, Sarah Adeky, and Katy Henio of the Ramah Weaver's Cooperative of Ramah, New Mexico; and Futures for Children of Albuquerque, New Mexico.

We have learned greatly from these people and organizations and, we hope, have accurately passed on the wisdom they have imparted to us. For wisdom and support of various kinds, we are also indebted to the following individuals:

Alix King; Martha Binford; Sara Voorhees (film critic and chief grip); Mary and Emory Sekaquaptewa; Fred Koots; Phyllis Witsell; Doris Ami and her family; Ruth and Ken Frazier; Nancy Stone and Lew Binford; Jill Beach; Glenn, Sandy, and Kerry Greene; Glenn Randolph; Rudy and Mary Jo Miller; Forrest and Sasha Furman; Pebbles, Benelda, Yvette, Bennie, and Mary Cohoe; Frank and Charlene Sanchez Reano and the Reano family; Robbie Miller; Tessie Naranjo; Phillip Coochyamptewa; Alph and Alfreda Secakuku; Ferrel Secakuku and his family; Phil Sekaquaptewa; Marlene and Alison Sekaquaptewa; Diana Shebala; Alonzo and Linda Quavehema and family; Autumn Borts; Dan and Frances Naminjgha; Anthony Ortiz; Diane Daffin; Crucita, JoAnn, Marlene, and Darlene Melcher and their families; Martha and Gene

Jackson; Alex and Ken Seoweta; Al and Josephine Slinkey; Glenibah Hardy; Jimmy and Irene Clark and Marie Salt-clah and their families; Jessie Caboni and her family; Mike Mitchell; Rodger Boyd; Bob and Bezo Morton; Jackie Bralove; Paul Conklin; Tim Seldes; Sam Vaughan; Victor Coochwytewa; Rene Ami; Nat Stone of the *Shim Messenger;* Ann Beckett; and Amy Nevitt.

Other individuals, for whom this book is in memoriam, are: Norma Ami; Abbott, Eugene, and Helen Sekaquaptewa; Kathleen Page; Mary Toya; Bill Toelle; Frank Stone; and Quiyo Page.

Superb and timely technical support was provided by Kristina and Joan Regan and David Corwell of Corrales Printing; Bill Parrish of Camera and Darkroom; Jayna Finch, Barbara Shaw, Chris Apadaca, and Alex Castrounis of Fox Photo; Tracy and Greg Baczkiewicz of Desert Photo; all hands at Carl's Color Lab; and Steve Donahue of Central Photographic in Albuquerque.

We are grateful for the support of Lily, Max, and Charlotte Hoffman and Kenny Page-Brooks, who helped in the final days of preparing this book; and Early Stone Ferguson; Nina and Thomas Kuntz; and Zack, Tyson, Caleb, and Grace Barrett, Sally Halvorson and Virginia Stone and Bazy Tankersley who (in the same period) graciously permitted themselves to be utterly ignored. As always, we are grateful to our daughters, Lindsey, Sally, Kendall, Dana, Lea, and Brooke, and their families.

We are grateful for the excellent help from people at Random House, who published an earlier version of this book: Ruth Fecych, Beth Thomas, Robbin Schiff, and Sabrina Bowers. We are most grateful to the people at Rio Nuevo Publishing who have given this book a Lazarus-like new life and a new look. This includes the welcoming Ross and Susan Humphreys, the publishers; Carrie Stusse and Lisa Anderson, gentle and careful wielders of the fine-toothed editorial comb; and designer Karen Schober, creator of this book's bold new look. Many thanks.

This book has been touched in one way or another by everyone listed here, and to them all we can only say thank you. We hope it does you all proud.

Some items pictured courtesy of the following organizations and individuals:

Adobe Gallery, Santa Fe and Albuquerque: pages 13, 52, 54, 58, 59, 60, 61 top, 62, 63, 64 top & bottom, 65, 69, 70, 72, 73 right, 74, 76 left & lower right, 81, 94 right, 110.

Bahti Indian Arts, Tucson and Santa Fe: pages 19, 26 left, 89, 95 right, 98 left, 120 right, 121.

Jill Beach: pages 27, 112.

Autumn Boris: page 77.

Case Trading Post, Santa Fe: pages 61 bottom, 66, 68, 80 left, 83 left & right, 120 left.

Garland's Indian Jewelry, Sedona: page 116.

Garland's Navajo Rugs, Sedona: pages 8, 18, 23, 32, 35, 37, 39, 90, 93.

Heard Museum Shop, Phoenix: pages 46, 50, 51, 53, 85, 95 left, 97, 98 right.

Hopi Fine Arts, Second Mesa: page 118 lower left.

Hubbell Trading Post, Ganado: pages 31, 38 right & left, 115 bottom right.

Maxwell Museum Shop, Albuquerque: pages 29, 57, 117.

Karen McCartney: page 119 top.

McGee's Native American Gallery, Holbrook: page 103.

Rudy and Mary Jo Miller: page 73 left.

Museum of Northern Arizona, Flagstaff: pages 87, 94 left.

Native Gold, Albuquerque: pages 108, 115 top right.

Palms Trading Company, Albuquerque: page 114 top.

The former Pueblo and Plains, Taos: pages 10, 20, 24, 71, 76 top right, 80 right, 106.

Richard Quam Jr.: page 41.

Ramah Navajo Weavers Association, Pine Hill: pages 25, 28.

Charlene Sanchez Reano: page 111.

The late Emory Sekaquaptewa: page 14.

Sonwai, Hotevilla: pages 119 bottom right.

Tanner Chaney Gallery, Albuquerque: pages 43, 105, 109, 113 top & bottom, 114 bottom, 115 left, 118 right & top left.

SUGGESTED READING

Adair, John. *The Navajo and Pueblo Silversmiths*. Norman, OK: University of Oklahoma Press, 1944, 1989.

Babcock, Barbara A., Guy Monthan, and Doris Monthan. *The Pueblo Storyteller: Development of a Figurative Ceramic Tradition*. Tucson, AZ: University of Arizona Press, 1986 (out of print).

Bahti, Mark. *A Guide to Navajo Sandpainting* (2nd ed.). Tucson, AZ: Rio Nuevo Publishers, 2000.

———. *Pueblo Stories and Storytellers*. Tucson, AZ: Rio Nuevo Publishers, 1996.

———. *Spirit in the Stone*. Tucson, AZ: Rio Nuevo Publishers, 1999.

Barnett, Franklin. *Dictionary of Prehistoric Indian Artifacts of the American Southwest*. Flagstaff, AZ: Northland Publishing, 1973 (out of print).

Bennett, Hal Zina. *Zuni Fetishes: Using Native American Sacred Objects for Meditation, Reflection, and Insight*. San Francisco, CA: Harper San Francisco, 1993.

Bennett, Noël. *Genuine Navajo Rug: How to Tell* (3rd ed.). Palmer Lake, CO: Filter Press, 2000.

Bennett, Noël, and Tiana Bighorse. *Navajo Weaving Way: The Path from Fleece to Rug*. Loveland, CO: Interweave Press, 1997.

———. *Working with the Wool: How to Weave a Navajo Rug*. Flagstaff, AZ: Northland Publishing, 1971 (out of print).

Berkholz, Richard C. *Old Trading Posts of the Four Corners: A Guide to Early-Day Trading Posts Established On or Around the Navajo, Hopi, and Ute Mountain Reservations*. Lake City, CO: Western Reflections Publishing Co., 2007.

Blair, Mary Ellen, and Laurence Blair. *The Legacy of a Master Potter: Nampeyo and Her Descendants*. Tucson, AZ: Rio Nuevo Publishers, 1999.

Cirillo, Dexter. *Southwestern Indian Jewelry*. New York: Abbeville Press, 1992.

Dalrymple, Larry. *Indian Basketmakers of the Southwest*. Santa Fe, NM: Museum of New Mexico Press, 2000.

David, Neil, Sr., J. Brent Ricks, and Alexander E. Antony, Jr. *Kachinas: Spirit Beings of the Hopi*. Albuquerque, NM: Avanyu Publishing, Inc., 1993.

Day, Jonathan S. *Traditional Hopi Kachinas: A New Generation of Carvers*. Flagstaff, AZ: Northland Publishing, 2000 (out of print).

Dedera, Don. *Artistry in Clay: Contemporary Pottery of the Southwest*. Flagstaff, AZ: Northland Publishing, 1985 (out of print).

———. *Navajo Rugs: The Essential Guide* (2nd rev. ed.). Flagstaff, AZ: Northland Publishing, 1996.

DeWald, Terry. *The Papago Indians and Their Basketry*. Tucson, AZ: Terry DeWald, 1979.

Dillingham, Rick. *Acoma and Laguna Pottery*. Santa Fe, NM: School of American Research Press, 1992.

———. *Fourteen Families in Pueblo Pottery*. Albuquerque, NM: University of New Mexico Press, 1994.

Dubin, Lois Sherr. *North American Indian Jewelry and Adornment: From Prehistory to the Present*. New York: Harry N. Abrams Inc., 1999 (concise ed. 2003).

Eddington, Patrick, and Susan Makov. *Trading Post Guidebook: Where to Find the Trading Posts, Galleries, Auctions, Artists, and Museums of the Four Corners Region*. Flagstaff, AZ: Northland Publishing, 1995 (out of print).

Finger, Judith, and Andrew D. Finger. *Circles of Life: Katsina Imagery on Hopi Wicker Basketry.* Ukiah, CA: Grace Hudson Museum & Sun House, 2006.

Gault, Ramona. *Artistry in Clay: A Buyer's Guide to Southwestern Indian Pottery.* Santa Fe, NM: Southwestern Association for Indian Arts, 1995.

Gibson, Daniel. *Pueblos of the Rio Grande: A Visitor's Guide.* Tucson, AZ: Rio Nuevo Publishers, 2001.

Indian Arts and Crafts Association (IACA) and Council for Indigenous Arts and Cultures (CIAC). *Collecting Authentic Indian Arts and Crafts: Traditional Work of the Southwest.* Summertown, TN: The Book Publishing Co., 1999.

Jacka, Jerry, and Nancy S. Hammack. *Indian Jewelry of the Prehistoric Southwest.* Tucson, AZ: University of Arizona Press, 1975.

Jacka, Lois Essary, and Jerry Jacka. *Beyond Tradition: Contemporary Indian Art and Its Evolution.* Flagstaff, AZ: Northland Publishing Company, 1988 (out of print).

———. *Navajo Jewelry: A Legacy of Silver and Stone.* Flagstaff, AZ: Northland Publishing, 1995 (out of print).

Kosik, Fran. *Native Roads: The Complete Motoring Guide to the Navajo and Hopi Nations.* Tucson, AZ: Rio Nuevo Publishers, 2005.

Kramer, Barbara. *Nampeyo and Her Pottery.* Tucson, AZ: University of Arizona Press, 2003.

Lamb, Susan. *A Guide to Navajo Rugs.* Tucson, AZ: Western National Parks Association, 1992.

LeFree, Betty. *Santa Clara Pottery Today.* Albuquerque, NM: University of New Mexico Press, 1975.

Lowell, Susan. *Navajo Rug Designs.* Tucson, AZ: Rio Nuevo Publishers, 2005.

Lowry, Joe Dan, and Joe P. Lowry. *Turquoise Unearthed: An Illustrated Guide.* Tucson, AZ: Rio Nuevo Publishers, 2002.

Marriott, Alice. *Maria: The Potter of San Ildefonso.* Norman, OK: University of Oklahoma Press, 1948, 1987.

McManis, Kent. *A Guide to Hopi Katsina Dolls.* Tucson, AZ: Rio Nuevo Publishers, 2000.

———. *Zuni Fetishes and Carvings* (expanded edition). Tucson, AZ: Rio Nuevo Publishers, 2004.

McManis, Kent, and Robert Jeffries. *A Guide to Navajo Weavings.* Tucson, AZ: Rio Nuevo Publishers, 1997.

Messier, Kim, and Pat Messier. *Hopi and Pueblo Tiles: An Illustrated History.* Tucson, AZ: Rio Nuevo Publishers, 2007.

Nahohai, Milford, and Elisa Phelps. *Dialogues with Zuni Potters.* Zuni, NM: Zuni A:Shiwi Publishing, 1995 (out of print).

Ostler, James, Marian Rodee, and Milford Nahohai. *Zuni: A Village of Silversmiths.* Zuni, NM: Zuni A:Shiwi Publishing, 1996 (out of print).

Peterson, Susan. *Lucy M. Lewis: American Indian Potter* (2nd ed.). New York: Kodansha International, distributed by Oxford University Press, 2004.

———. *Pottery by American Indian Women: The Legacy of Generations.* New York: Abbeville Press, 1997.

Reichard, Gladys A. *Spider Woman: A Story of Navajo Weavers and Chanters.* Albuquerque, NM: University of New Mexico Press, 1997.

Robinson, Alambert E. *The Basket Weavers of Arizona.* Albuquerque, NM: University of New Mexico Press, 1954, 1991 (out of print).

Rodee, Marian E. *One Hundred Years of Navajo Rugs.* Albuquerque, NM: University of New Mexico Press, 1995.

Rodee, Marian, and James Ostler. *The Fetish Carvers of Zuni* (rev.). Albuquerque, NM: Maxwell Museum of Anthropology/University of New Mexico; and Zuni, NM: Pueblo of Zuni Arts and Crafts, 1995.

Secakuku, Alph. *Following the Sun and Moon: Hopi Kachina Tradition.* Flagstaff, AZ: Northland Publishing, in cooperation with the Heard Museum, 1995.

Simpson, Georgiana Kennedy. *Navajo Ceremonial Baskets: Sacred Symbols Sacred Space.* Summertown, TN: The Book Publishing Co., 2003.

Tanner, Clara Lee. *Apache Indian Baskets.* Tucson, AZ: University of Arizona Press, 1982.

Teiwes, Helga. *Hopi Basket Weaving: Artistry in Natural Fibers.* Tucson, AZ: University of Arizona Press, 1996.

———. *Kachina Dolls: The Art of Hopi Carvers.* Tucson, AZ: University of Arizona Press, 1991.

Tisdale, Shelby J. *Fine Indian Jewelry of the Southwest: The Millicent Rogers Museum Collection.* Santa Fe, NM: Museum of New Mexico Press, 2006.

Toulouse, Betty. *Pueblo Pottery of the New Mexico Indians: Ever Constant, Ever Changing.* Santa Fe, NM: Museum of New Mexico Press, 1977.

Trimble, Stephen. *Talking with the Clay: The Art of Pueblo Pottery.* Santa Fe, NM: School of American Research Press, 1993.

Washburn, Dorothy K., ed. *The Elkus Collection: Southwestern Indian Art.* San Francisco, CA: California Academy of Sciences; distributed by University of Washington Press (Seattle), 1984 (out of print).

Wheat, Joe Ben. *Blanket Weaving in the Southwest.* Tucson, AZ: University of Arizona Press, 2003.

Whiteford, Andrew Hunter. *Southwestern Indian Baskets: Their History and Their Makers.* Santa Fe, NM: School of American Research Press; distributed by University of Washington Press (Seattle), 1988.

Wright, Barton. *Classic Hopi and Zuni Kachina Figures.* Santa Fe, NM: Museum of New Mexico Press, 2006.

———. *Clowns of the Hopi: Tradition Keepers and Delight Makers.* Flagstaff, AZ: Northland Publishing, 1994.

———. *Hopi Kachinas: The Complete Guide to Collecting Kachina Dolls* (rev.). Flagstaff, AZ: Northland Publishing, 2000.

———. *Kachinas: A Hopi Artist's Documentary.* Paintings by Cliff Bahnimptewa. Flagstaff, AZ: Northland Publishing, in cooperation with the Heard Museum, 1973.

Wright, Margaret Nickelson. *Hopi Silver: The History and Hallmarks of Hopi Silversmithing.* Albuquerque, NM: University of New Mexico Press, 2003.

INDEX

Page numbers in **bold** type indicate illustrations.

A

Acoma Pueblo, 22, 60
    pottery, **54, 56,** 57, **59, 60, 61**
    visiting, 124
agriculture:
    ceremonies of, 21, 22
    in prehistory, 17, 19, 25, 42
Aguilar, Wayne, **113**
Akimel O'odham (Pima), 19, 25, 95, 97
    basketry, 95
Anasazi, 19, 20, 22
    jewelry, 102
    pottery, 54, 61
animal motifs:
    fetishes, **43, 44**-45, 111, **116, 117**
    in fetishes vs. carvings, 41-43, 45
    figurines, **6,** 14, **25, 29,** 73, 75, 102
    and heartlines, 44, 59, 73, 83
    katsinas, 50, 53
    in pottery, 62, 63, 70, 79
    sacred colors and directions of, 43, 44
    storytellers, 62
Apaches, 17, 22, 25-29, 32
    basketry, 88, **89, 90**
    jewelry, **120**
    traditions of, 26-28
    visiting, 128
arts and crafts
    documentation of, 11
    fakes and imitations, 11-12

    federal regulation of, 11, 12, 47, 105, 108, 109
    imported components of, 12
    machine-made, 10, 11, 104, 107, 109
    prices of, 11, 12
    supplies (findings) for, 104, 105, 107
    use of term, 8-9

B

basketry, 85-99
    Apache, **8,** 88, **89, 90**-91
    burden, **89**
    buyers' tips, 88-89
    coiling, 87-88, **93, 94,** 95, 98
    dyes, 85, 86, 91, 94
    fakes and imitations, 11, 88
    friendship dance, **97**
    Havasupai, 92, **93**
    Hopi, **26, 85,** 86, **87,** 88, **94**
    horsehair, 98
    methods of making, 86-88
    Navajo, 88, 94-**95**
    O'odham, **19,** 88, **95, 97, 98**
    Papago. *See* O'odham
    Pima. *See* O'odham
    plaited wicker, 94
    plaques, **85,** 86, **87, 94**
    in prehistory, 19, 85-88
    San Juan Paiute, 88, 95, **98**
    sifter, **26**
    stitches, 86-88, **98**
    twining, 86-87
    wedding, **95,** 98
    wire, 97
    Yuman, 88

beadwork:
  drilling, **102,** 110
  heishi, 11, 45, 104, 110, 111, 117
  prehistoric, 100, 102
  Santo Domingo, **106,** 110-111
Beaver, Bill, 98
Begay, Mary Lee, **38**
belt buckles, 111, **118**
Betoney, Billy, **103,** 104
blackware, **6, 10, 25,** 59, 71, **72, 73,** 75, **76, 77**
blankets:
  chief, 32
  saddle, 32, 38
bolas. *See* bolos
bolos, 111
Boone, Lena, **117**
Borts, Autumn, 77
bow guards, **113,** 114
bracelets:
  cluster, 113-114, 115
  friendship, **121**
  height, 120
  Hopi overlay, **14,** 118
  silver and stone, **113, 114**

C

carvings, 41-53
  fetishes vs., 41-43
  figurines, 14, **29,** 75, 102
  Hopi katsina dolls, 11, 45-53. *Also see* katsina dolls
  Zuni "fetishes," **41, 43, 44**
  Zuni katsina dolls, 53
Cata, Rosita, **74**
ceramics. *See* pottery

channel inlay, **115,** 117
Charley, Herman, **112**
Chavez, Ronald, **109**
Cheromiah, Evelyn, 70
Chino, Marie, 59
Chiricahua Apache, 26, 27, 28, 29, 89
churro wool, **24,** 32, 35
Clark, Carl and Irene, **105**
Cling, Alice, **57**
clown katsinas, **50,** 52-53
Cochiti Pueblo, 22, 62-63
  history of, 62
  pottery, **3, 62**
  storytellers, **3, 62**
  visiting, 126
concha belts, **112,** 117
Conn, Tina, **32**
Coochwytewa, Victor, **26**
Coochyamtewa, Phillip, **47**
coral, 110
Cordero, Helen, **62**
Coriz, Doris and James Del, **27**
cotton wrap, 110
cradle dolls, 46, **47**
cross necklaces, 113

D

Da, Popovi, 71
Da, Tony, 73
Day, Chalmers, **118**
Del Coriz, Doris and James, **27**
Deyuse, Leekya, 117
documentation, 11
dolls. *See* katsina dolls

E

earrings:
  Hopi overlay, **118**
  inlaid, **109**
  joclas, 110
  mosaic, **5**
Evans, Desbah, **35**

F

fakes and imitations, 11-12
  basketry, 88
  jewelry, 104-109
  katsina dolls, 11, 51
  weaving, 37-38
Feather Woman (Helen Naha), **65**
Fendenheim, James, **120**
fetish carvings, 41-45
  heartlines of, 44
  necklaces, 11, 45, 111, **116, 117**
  vs. spiritual fetishes, 43, 45
  stones used for, 45
  Zuni, **5, 41, 43, 44,** 45
figurines,
  animal, **6,** 14, **25, 29,** 73, 75, 102
  Mudheads, 10
fine arts, 121
folk art, 10
Fragua, Juanita, **68**

G

Garcia, Alvina, **79**
Garcia, Stephanie, **98**
Gaspar, Dinah and Pete, **116**

gold jewelry, 107, **108, 115, 119**
Gonzalez, Rose, 71
grandmother necklace, **27,** 111
greenware, 57, 58, 61
Griego, Eleanor Pina, **81**
Gutierrez, Dorothy and Paul, **6, 10**

H

Hakataya culture, 20
Haloo, Nancy, **100**
Hano, 64
Hardy, Glenibah, **18**
Havasupai, 20, 88, 92
  basketry, 92, **93**
  traditions of, 92
  visiting, 127
heishi beadwork, 11, 45, 104, 110, 111, 117
Henio, Jaymes, **28**
Henry, Wilfred, **114**
Hisatsinom, 19. *See also* Anasazi, Hopi
Hohokam culture, 19, 100
  jewelry, 100-102
Home of the Elder Brother, 97
Hopi, 19, 48
  basketry, **26, 85, 86, 87,** 88, **94**
  history of, 48
  katsina dolls, 45-53, **46, 47, 50, 51, 52, 53**
  language of, 48
  pottery, **63, 64, 65**
  silver overlay, **14, 26,** 117, **118**-119
  villages of, 9, 48, 63, 64, 94
  visiting, 124
  weaving, 31-32
Hualapai, 20, 91
  basketry, 91

visiting, 127

I

IACA. *See* Indian Arts and Crafts Association
Indian Arts and Crafts Association, 8, 10, 37, 104,
    109
"Indian handmade," 11, 104
"Indian made" or "constructed" or "assembled," 104
Indians,
    land of, 15-16
    prehistory of, 17-20
    tribal sovereignty of, 15, 22
    use of term, 8
    See also specific tribes
ironwood, 120
Isleta Pueblo, 66-67
    pottery, **66**
    visiting, 125
ivory, fossilized, 45, 117, 120

J

Jemez Pueblo, 67-68
    pottery, 67, **68**
    visiting, 126
jewelry, 100-121
    Apache, **120**
    beads and mosaic (Santo Domingo), **5, 20,
    27, 106, 109, 110, 111**
    buyers' tips, 104-107
    channel inlay (Zuni), **115,** 117
    cluster, 113-114, 115
    drilling of, 102
    fetish necklaces (Zuni), 45, **116, 117**
    findings for, 104

gold, 107, **108, 115, 119**
"Indian handmade," 104
"Indian made" or "constructed" or
"assembled," 104
new directions, 119-121
pawn, 113
prehistoric, 19, 100-102
silver (O'odham), **120, 121**
silver and stones (Navajo), **112, 113, 114**
silver and stones (Zuni), **100, 114, 115,
116, 117**
silver overlay (Hopi), **14, 26,** 117, **118,**
119
turquoise, 107-109, 112
Jicarilla Apache, 26, 27, 90
    basketry, 90-91
    visiting, 128
joclas earrings/necklaces, 110
Joseyesva, Farron, **118**

K

Kabotie, Fred, 118
kachinas. *See* katsinas
Kalestewa, Jack, **83**
katsina dances, 22, 45, 46, 47, 51, 52, 53
katsina dolls, 45, **46,** 47-50, **51, 52, 53**
    butterfly, **51**
    categories of, 51-53
    chief figures, 51-52
    clown figures, **50,** 52-53
    collecting, 49-51
    cradle, 46, **47**
    criteria for, 50-51
    Crow Mother, 51
    Eototo, 52

fakes, 11, 51
guard figures, 52
identity of, 50
Katsin-mana, **52**
Kocha Honaw, **53**
Koyaala, 53
Masau'u, 52
materials for, 46-47, 50
mudheads, 52-53
ogres, 52
prices of, 11, 50
Sikyaqoqlo, **46**
stomachache, 49
women, 52
Zuni, 53
katsinas (spirits), 22, 45, 46, 47, 51-53
knickknacks, 10
Koshare (clowns), 22, 53
Kowemy, Wendell, **69**
Koyaala katsinas, 53

L

Laguna Pueblo, 68-69
    history of, 22, 66, 68-69
    pottery, **13, 69**-70
    traditions of, 69
    visiting, 125
lapis lazuli, 45, 110, 120
Lesou (pottery maker), 63
Lewis, Carolyn, **37**
Lewis, Lucy, **56,** 59
Lewis, Sharon, **61**
Lewis, T., **51**
Loco, Jan, **120**
Loloma, Charles, **119**-120

loom, upright, 31, 36, 37, 38
lost-wax castings, 104
Lovato, Ray, **106**

M

malachite, 45, 120
Man in the Maze, **95,** 97, **120**
Manuel, Frances, **95**
Manuel, Rick, **121**
Maquina, Corn, **25**
Martinez, Elsie, **24**
Martinez, Julian, 71, **72**
Martinez, Maria, 71, **72, 73**
Mescalero Apache, 26, 27, 29
    basketry, 88
    visiting, 128
Mimbres, 20
    pottery, 20, 59
Mogollon culture, 20, 22, 54, 102
    jewelry, 102
    pottery, 54
Montoya, Eudora, 75
mosaic, Santo Domingo, **111**
Mudheads:
    in basketry, **94**
    figurines, **10**
    katsinas, 52-53

N

Naha, Helen (Feather Woman), **65**
Naha, Regina, **50**
Naha, Victoria, **114**
Nambe Pueblo, 22
    visiting, 127

Nampeyo (pottery maker), 63
Nampeyo, James Garcia, **64**
Naranjo, Celestina, **76**
Navajo tribe, 15, 26, 33-34
    basketry, 88, 94-**95**
    figurines, **29**
    pottery, **57, 70**
    sandpaintings, 23, 33, 34, 35
    silver and stone jewelry, **103, 105, 112,**
    113, 114
    visiting, 128
    weaving, **18, 23, 24, 28, 31, 32,** 34, **35,**
    36, **37, 38**
necklaces:
    bead-and-tab, 111
    beadwork, **106,** 110-111
    bolos, 111
    chiclet, 111
    cotton wrap for, 110
    cross, 113
    Depression, **110**
    fetish (Zuni), 11, 45, **116, 117**
    "grandmother," **27,** 111
    joclas, 110
    Navajo styles, 112-113
    Santo Domingo styles, **20, 106, 110, 111**
    squash blossom, 112-113, **114**
    Zuni-style, **103**
needlepoint style, 115
Nequatewa, Verma, **119**
nickel-silver jewelry, 104, 107, 114

O
ollas, 56
O'odham people, 14, 19, 25, 96-97. *See also* Akimel
    O'odham, Tohono O'odham

basketry, **19,** 88, **95, 97, 98**
silversmiths, **120, 121**
visiting, 127-128
overlay, silver, **14, 26,** 117, **118,** 119, **120, 121**
Owen, Angie Reano, **20,** 111

P

Padilla, Andrew, **13**
Paiute. *See* San Juan Paiute
Papago. *See* Tohono O'odham
pawn, 113
pendants, 100, 102
    Hopi, **118**
    Navajo, **108,** 112-113
    Santo Domingo, 110, **111**
    Zuni, **115**
petit point style, 115
Peynetsa, Anderson and Avelia, **83**
Piaso, Thompson, **113**
Picuris Pueblo, 70
    pottery, **71**
    visiting, 127
Pima. *See* Akimel O'odham
pins, Zuni, 115
Plains Indians, 32, 112
plaques. *See* basketry
Pojoaque Pueblo, 22
    visiting, 127
pottery, 54-83
    Acoma, **54, 56, 59, 60, 61**
    Anasazi, 54, 61
    blackware, **6, 10, 25,** 59, 71, **72, 73,** 75,
    76, 77
    buyers' tips, 57-59
    Cochiti, **3, 62**

coil and scrape method, 56, 58
corrugated, 61
curing of, 56
"egg," **76**
ethnographic wear of, 59
fireclouds on, **57**
greenware, 57, 58, 61
handcrafted vs. handmade, 58
Hopi, **63, 64, 65**
inlay in, 71
Isleta, **66**
Jemez, 67, **68**
kiln-fired, 57, 58, 59, 83
kiva design, **71, 74, 80, 83**
Laguna, **13, 69**-70
methods and materials for, 56-57
Mimbres, 20, 59
Navajo, **57, 70**
ollas, 56
Picuris, **71**
polychrome, 54, 59, 74
prehistoric, 20, 54
prices of, 59
San Ildefonso, 71-**72, 73**
San Juan, **74**
Santa Ana, 74-75
Santa Clara, **6,** 75-**76, 77**
Santo Domingo, 78-**79**
sgraffito, 73, 75, **76**
slip of, 57, 59, 62, 63, 66, 67, 71, 74, 78, 79, 81, 83
Taos, 79-**80**
temper of, 56, 61, 69, 75, 79, 81, 83
Zia, 75, **81**-82
Zuni, **1, 58, 83**
prehistory, 17-20

Pueblo Revolt, 21-22
Pueblo tribes, 19, 20-25, 56
    clown tradition of, 22
    creation stories of, 23, 31
    kivas of, 21, 45
    languages of, 22
    as matrilineal, 22
    moieties of, 22
    visiting, 122-127

Q

Quam, Richard, Jr., **41**
Quandelacy family, 45
Quirana (clowns), 22
Quotskuyva, Dextra, 63, **64**

R

rainbirds, 83
Ramah reservation weaving, 35
Reano, Charlene Sanchez, **5, 111**
Reano, Charlotte Sanchez, 111
Reano, Frank, **5**
Reano, Percy, **106**
Reano Owen, Angie, **20,** 111
Roan, Emma, **31**
rugs, Navajo, 32-39
    Burntwater design, **31**
    churro wool, **24**
    Crystal, **18**
    Eyedazzlers, 34
    Ganado Red, **35**
    Old Style, **38**
    pictorials, 35
    sandpainting, **23,** 35

stitches of, **38**
Storm Pattern, **32**
Teec Nos Pos, **38**
Tree of Life, 35, **39**
Two Grey Hills, **37**
Wide Ruins, **31**
yei, Yei-be-chei, **28,** 35

S

Salt River Pima-Maricopa, 95
    visiting, 128
Sanchez, Russell, **73**
Sand Papago, 96
Sandia Pueblo, 23
    visiting, 125
San Felipe Pueblo, 22
    visiting, 126
San Ildefonso Pueblo, 22, 71
    pottery, 71-**72, 73**
    visiting, 126
San Juan Paiute, 99
    basketry, 88, 95, **98**
    visiting, 128
San Juan Pueblo, 22, 73
    pottery, **74**
    visiting, 127
Santa Ana Pueblo, 22, 74-75
    pottery, 74-75
    visiting, 126
Santa Clara Pueblo, 22, 76
    figurines, **6, 10, 25,** 75
    pottery, 75-**76, 77**
    visiting, 126
Santo Domingo Pueblo, 78
    beads and mosaic jewelry, **5, 20, 27, 106,**

        109, 110, 111
    languages of, 22
    pottery, 78-**79**
    visiting, 125
Secakuku, Alph, 118
Secakuku, Kevin, **53**
Sekaquaptewa, Emory, **14,** 46
Sena, Ralph, **71**
sgraffito style, 73, 75, **76**
Shebola, Darren, **5**
Sheche family, **44**
shell jewelry, 11, 19, 100, 102, 110, 111, 117
Sikyatki pottery, 63
silver:
    Hopi overlay, 117, **118,** 119
    Navajo jewelry, **103, 105, 112, 113, 114**
    O'odham, **120, 121**
    sand-casting of, 112
    Santo Domingo jewelry, **106, 109, 110, 111**
    soldering of, 107, 113, 117, 118
    stamping, 14, 112, **113,** 118
    weight of, 118
    Zuni jewelry, **100,** 107, 113, **114, 115**
silver-fill jewelry, 104
Simplicio, Mike, **115**
singing, 10
Southwest:
    Indian lands in, 15-16, **21**
    map, **9**
    prehistoric cultures, 17-20
    tribal areas in eighteenth century in, 21
    use of term, 8
Southwestern Association for Indian Arts, 104
Spider Woman/Spider Grandmother, 31, 36
squash blossom:

necklaces, 112-113, **114**
Stevens, Frances, **19**
stitches:
 basketry, 86-88
 weaving, 35, **38**
stones:
 cluster style, 113-114, 115
 inlaid on inside of jewelry, **119**, 120
 needlepoint, 115
 petit point, 115
storytellers, **3,** 10, **62,** 67, **80**
SWAIA. *See* Southwestern Association for Indian
 Arts

T

tabs (beads), 111
Tafoya, Emily, **76**
Tafoya, Margaret, 75
Tafoya family, **76**
Taos Pueblo, 22, 80-81
 pottery, 79-**80**
 visiting, 127
Tapia, Belen, **76**
Teller, Stella, **66**
Tenakhongva, Clark, **46**
Tenario, Karen, **80**
Tesuque Pueblo, 22
 visiting, 126
Tewawina, Pat, **118**
Tohono O'odham (Papago), 19, 96-97
 basketry, **19, 95, 97, 98**
 silversmiths, **120, 121**
 traditional symbols, 97
 visiting, 127
Torivio, Dorothy, **54, 59, 61**

tortoise-shell, 115
Toya, Mary, 10, 67
Tree of Life motif, 35, **39**
Trujillo, Leonard and Mary, **3**
Tsinnie, Shirley, **38**
Tso, Luanna, **23**
Tsosie, Boyd, **108**
Tsosie, Evelyn, **39**
turquoise jewelry, 107-109, 112
 block (plastic), 109
 chalk, 109
 cluster bracelets and rings, 113-114, 115
 color of, 107, 108, 109
 grades of, 108-109
 healing and protective powers of, 112
 hot needle test of, 109
 imported foreign, 108
 matrix of, 108
 mosaic work, 111
 natural, 108-109
 raw, 111
 reconstituted, 109
 spiderweb, 108
 squash blossom, 112-113, **114**
 stabilized, 109
 treated, 109

W

Walapai. *See* Hualapai
Warren, Homer, **29**
water jars (Western Apache), 89
water serpent motif, 71, 75
water symbols, 67, 81
weaving, 31-39
 buyers' tips, 36-38

chief blankets, 32
churro wool for, **24,** 32, 35
criteria for, 36
design motifs for, 34-35
dyes for, 34, 36, 37
fakes of, 11, 37-38
Navajo rugs, 31-39. *Also see* rugs, Navajo
in prehistory, 19
sashes, 31
stitches, **38**
wedding baskets, Navajo, **95,** 98
wedding vases, **13, 68, 76**
Western Apache, 26, 27, 89
basketry, **8, 89, 90**
visiting, 128
water jars, 89
wire basketry, 97

cluster bracelets, 113-114, 115
jewelry, **100, 114, 115, 116, 117**
katsina dolls, 53
pottery, **1, 58, 83**
visiting, 124

Y

Yavapai, 20
Yazzie, Angie, **80**
yei-be-chei. *See* yeis
yeis:
images on jewelry, **105**
images on pottery, 70
images in weaving, **28,** 35
Yuman tribes, 20, 25, 96

Z

Zia Pueblo, 82
pottery, **81**-82
visiting, 126
Zuni tribe, 42-43
carvings, **5, 41, 43, 44,** 45